How to Leave an Asshole

A Practical Guide on How to Heal from a Toxic Relationship and #leavetheasshole

This book is presented for educational and entertainment purposes only. The information provided in this book is not a substitute for professional advice or therapy. The author makes no legal claims, and the material is not intended to replace the services of a certified professional. The author and publisher are not offering this book and its contents as legal, health or other professional services advice and make no representations or warranties of any kind nor assume liabilities of any kind for damages resulting from the use of information contained therein which is based on the author's personal opinions, research and observations. Although every precaution has been taken in the preparation of this book, the publisher and author assume no responsibility for errors or omissions. The author and publisher recommend you seek advice from a medical professional if you are looking to make any lifestyle changes.

Cover art by Oladimeji Alaka
Format Design by Deepak Gupta (fiverr.com/weformat)

PO Box 192

Brevard NC 28712

ISBN: 978-0-578-40791-3

This book is dedicated to all those who believe they will never heal or be whole again. May this heartache and pain be the source of your greatest spiritual awakening.

"The wound is the place where the light enters you."
Rumi

For my son, Matt. I'm so proud of the man you have become.
I love you!

Contents

Introduction

Wanker. Dickhead.

Prick. Douchebag.

They go by different names in various parts of the world. But assholes all share one thing in common: they all act the same. They have the same traits and predictably follow the exact same "textbook" patterns as if operating out of the exact same manual, yep.

And they're everywhere. Geez, they're everywhere. They're in the workplace, they live next door to you, they sit across from you in school, they're shopkeepers of businesses you frequent, and they're even in your own family.

Before we go further, let's clarify out of the gate the focus of *this* book is assholes with whom we've fallen in love with romantically, and from whom – oops - we find we need to untangle ourselves from and heal. Sadly, most of us have fallen for at least one at some point along our journey.

And if you're like me and you've unfortunately fallen in love with an asshole, or dated one, or God-help-you married one or come close to marrying one, then you're already all too familiar with the havoc that is wreaked on your life and wellbeing. My heart goes out to you.

(Important side note: Admittedly by habit, I tend to assume most of my readers are women. That's whom I've had the most interaction with during my own personal journey to healing. This precious group of women I've come to know and love have shared their own struggles and determination to heal. However, if you're a man reading this book - no matter if you're dealing with an asshole who is a man *or* woman - all the shared advice here still holds true for you, too. None of us are immune. So, please forgive my occasional inclination to speak directly to women at times in this book; it is done so out of habit.)

So anyway, yeah, I got involved with a guy "like that" and fell in love. He was sweet and sexy and handsome and I never thought I'd someday call myself a survivor because of him. I didn't think he was an asshole or a guy "like that" until I was in too deep. I was hooked. And, getting over him was the hardest thing I've ever had to do in my life.

No, I'm not a stupid woman. I promise you I do not have low self-esteem. I've never secretly harbored a desire to be abused. None of us do. More often than not, we find ourselves romantically in-too-deep with assholes because we're guilty of one thing: being an empath. More on empaths later.

It's important to note, I refer to our problem partners as "assholes" in this book, but the more clinical term is "narcissists." Google the term and then brace yourself and know this: *An educated empath is the only person who can survive a narcissist.* I'm no mental health professional, but after reading countless books, studying the opinions of dozens of experts, watching hundreds of videos on the topic, interviewing countless people, chatting with thousands of women going through their own journeys of healing, and years spent in one-on-one counseling myself, I will tell you *"narcissist"* is the more accepted label given to the assholes we're dealing with.

There are varying degrees to how bad they can be and they come in a wide spectrum of severity. Some are complete assholes. Some are the simple, somewhat harmless garden variety type. Some are merely slightly irregular people. And, some are of the Voldemort ilk.

Life with them is an amusement park ride (alternating joy and excitement with fear and white knuckles) and questioning your own sanity in signing up for the ride to begin with (cue music: Love Rollercoaster).

This book examines getting away and healing from the very worst kinds of narcissists and assholes.

> *"Hmmm… I'm not sure if my guy rises to the level of being a narcissist/asshole."*

If you wonder whether your partner is a narcissist, this book will help you identify if they are part of this category. Once equipped with this information, you will be able to take the next steps and protect yourself if they are, indeed, an asshole. No one deserves to unwittingly find themselves in an unhealthy situation that may become abusive. I dare say, most abusive relationships can be avoided, because all assholes and narcissists exhibit the same red flag behaviors if you know what to look for. Sadly, most narcissists will eventually become abusive.

> *"Actually, I already know I'm with an asshole. Now what?"*

If you're already certain that you're in deep with an asshole, this book will help you escape and fully heal from the experience. This book shares what I learned along my own path to healing, what worked for me, and lessons learned along the way. If you are my closest friend, this is the advice I would share with you.

Just know, this will be no ordinary breakup. Breaking up with a narcissist – especially a raging narcissist - is never easy. It will be a life-changing harrowing experience, but there is hope.

Many other women (and men) have been through exactly what you're going through, have survived and successfully found happiness again. Rest assured, we know what you're feeling. The desperation, the fear, the sense of loss, betrayal, confusion, and loneliness, we know it all.

Breathe deeply, this book is for you.

You will learn how to detach from your narcissist/asshole and heal from the whole mess so you are whole and healthy again (mentally, physically, spiritually, emotionally) and come out the other side with your heart more open and loving than ever before. You will overcome the worst your asshole dishes out, stay strong through the process, reset your life and find a stronger healthier you... and yes, even love again. This horrible experience will be the very source of your greatest spiritual awakening, like it was for me.

If you're someone who has loved a narcissist and has already successfully escaped, you know healing is not a linear process. It takes a long time and it's a daily struggle. The sadness comes and goes, you struggle some days and other days are better. Some days you want to fold and fall to your knees, tired of being in survival mode. Other days you are determined and hit the floor running.

Recovering from an asshole involves dealing with unresolved anger and emotions that are hard to shake. The trauma bond you have with your narcissist will make you feel a fraction of the glorious person you are. You will feel re-victimized by people who don't understand narcissistic abuse. Family members and friends will not understand. You will be attacked by your asshole's friends and family who will harass you on behalf of the asshole (these folks are commonly referred to in the healing community as flying monkeys). You will be confused as to how you even got here. The effects of narcissistic abuse are annihilating and long-lasing.

I get it, sweet girl. I know where you are emotionally and will share with you how I coped with the exact same struggle, and survived.

Throughout my healing I consulted therapists, abuse experts, my personal doctor and chatted with women just like me. I've also talked to men going through their own nightmare. I've also read and researched and explored every natural way to healing that I could find. I'll share all of it, everything what worked for me in an easy to follow plan. Feel free to pick and choose what you believe will work for you. I offer you all the details of the path I took as you begin your journey.

Is this book for you?

This book is for you if, like me, you desire these things in your life:

1. a deep sense of peace
2. love again (in the form of healthy relationship)
3. balance in life
4. a stronger spiritual connection
5. and, to never again go through such a horrible situation such as this, ever *EVER* again.

This book is NOT for you if these two statements apply:

- <u>You are weirded out by talk of spiritual matters, the universe, God and/or natural healing modalities</u>.

  I'm a big fan of meditation, acupuncture, reiki, tapping, vinyasa yoga, qigong yoga, chakra balancing, crystals, essential oils, and other things (that are admittedly "woo-woo" by many people's definition). A large part of my healing was spiritual in nature.

  My definition of wellbeing and good health means having a spirit of peace and love, having a grateful heart, getting good sleep, being authentic, having joy in my life, having clarity and focus, and healthy relationships. Everything I did - including the woo-woo stuff and traditional means - led to those things.

- <u>You aren't willing to look at your own junk and put in the work to be a better person.</u> (i.e. you're an asshole – ha!)

> Basically, if you're not a doer, you won't get much from this book. If you want someone else to do all the work for you, this book isn't for you. If you want to blame everyone else for your life, this book is not for you. If you're an "I can't" kind of person, or are whiney and want to unpack and live in the "I'm a victim" space, this book is not for you. You aren't ready to live asshole-free. Come back later.

However, if those two statements ***don't*** apply to you, then this book will guide you how to get over an asshole, escape and heal, teach you the invisible threshold to getting healthy, and the one and only key to restoring your relationship with your asshole to a healthy one (if it's possible).

You will learn how to take this horrible experience in your life and use it to bring you peace and a loving future. You'll even come to the point where you're thankful that it happened (*gasp*, I know… I bet you a cup of coffee you will, though). I got through my ordeal, healed and can even laugh about it now (and not in a fake laugh kind of way).

Listen, this is what the universe wants for you: peacekeeping and love. And your experience can and will be the source of your greatest spiritual awakening if you allow it. No more fear and confusion. No more weakness. Fewer wobble moments that un-nerve you. Get rid of the past and burn up those old emotions and accept what has happened. Focus on it, face it head on, feel it through and do the work of loving yourself. This is the path to healing!

So, grab what works for you from these pages. Be open-minded to everything and closed-minded to nothing. Ground yourself in self-care as we set off on this journey and you will come out the other side with a heart more supple than ever before. You deserve to be whole, happy and peaceful.

In the end, I hope this book also gives bystanders, friends and family an understanding of loved ones in toxic and abusive relationships. It's important to know what to do and what NOT to do and say to loved ones who are in the grips of an asshole.

The good news is, if you're still reading right now, your healing process has already begun. You're ready for wellness and happiness.

Keep the faith and let's get on with it. If it makes you feel better, feel free to raise your middle finger to all the assholes and flying monkeys we're leaving behind as we set off on this journey.

My hope is that you will gain a new outlook on life, a plan and excitement for the future while at the same time honoring who you are at your core.

Let's go!

Chapter 1
Before We Get Started

As we are about to set off on this journey, please promise me three things:

1. Promise to show up.

Every day. And, promise yourself you'll *keep* showing up. There will be days when you don't feel like dealing with any of this. That's normal. You'll feel hopeless, exhausted, and scared. You will be a barely-here, beautiful mess. That's all okay and to be expected. Come as you are, every day. Let's take this life-changing journey together.

2. Stay strong through the hard stuff.

Pain and sadness and all the rest are valid human responses to what's happening to us. It's hard working our way through these emotions. It's also hard not to hate assholes. How can you not feel anger and disgust toward someone who hurts us, disrespects us, takes our money, sets their flying monkeys on us when we leave and then seems to laugh and smirk that they've brought us to our knees? Why wouldn't anyone hate someone like that? Unpacking at that place is not the answer.

The threshold to healing is actually the very place where you face those most painful experiences that hurt us the most, feeling it all deeply. You have to commit to the adage, "There is no victory without a struggle."

We have to be okay with the struggle.

3. And, promise to persevere.

Do. Not. Quit. And if you do feel like quitting follow the advice laid out here for you (Chapter 9: On the Brink of Desperation – Triage Plan). ☺

Sweet girl, you deserve a do-over, a life reset. You deserve to regain the control in your life. You deserve love and peace. We will heal you from top to bottom from your trip-up with an asshole. You will heal and become whole again, I promise. You will never be shackled ever again. Okay? Good! Onward…

Chapter 2
The First "What the f...?"

It'll come, love. More likely, it already has if you've felt the need to pick up this book. I'm talking about that very first "What the...?" moment when you do a double-take and ask yourself if you *really* did see and hear what you *think* you saw and heard - something bewildering your asshole does or says that leaves you completely speechless.

For me, it all started slowly with something as simple as buying groceries and putting them in the refrigerator wrong. "He" was extremely annoyed by how I had unloaded the groceries. I had apparently messed things up by not following the system that was in place (and of which, my bad, I wasn't aware). I had to remove everything (admittedly a load of stuff, because I'm a foodie and cook a lot, but I digress) and place them back correctly this time. I had screwed up and he was irritated. That was the first very small glimmer I had of his need for control over every aspect of our lives.

"Really?"... I thought to myself.

It seemed crazy to me that someone could be angered by something so trivial. I could see someone maybe being *slightly* annoyed by someone messing up their system, but did it warrant the level of irritation and anger he seemed to be showing? The ridiculousness of the whole scenario seemed almost funny to me (although I would later learn his anger was nothing to laugh at). Surely, he was joking… or wasn't thinking correctly… or he must be under stress. I began to rationalize to make sense of it. "*Yes, that's it, of course that's it.*"

And, I scolded myself for not seeing the obvious from the start: "*Really, how sloppy and disrespectful of me to mess things up by being so utterly reckless with the groceries. Yes, of course, there's an assigned spot for cheese and a spot for the root beer and a correct shelf for deli meats. My goodness, have some class, girl!*" This was, after all, his life… and I was fitting into it.

And there were other red flags (warning signs) that I chose to shrug off and explain away. Someone had carved "FU" in the stone pavers that lead up to his house. "*What the…?*" I wondered who in the world would ever do such a thing. That's a lot of anger for someone to take the time and effort to carve that into rock. To this day, I never asked him who did it. I assumed it surely must have been a mistake. Whomever had done it had gotten the wrong house, I assumed.

And he told me about his previous relationships. He spoke ill of all the women in his past. His ex-wife was a monster who stole money from him. His ex-fiancé was a "gold digger" and at one time had him paying to fly her ex-husband all over the world. Her kids were also ill-behaved and were going to cause him to be sued. He also told me he had been falsely accused of sexual harassment by a female employee at work and he settled the lawsuit for a large sum of money, again the victim of another gold-digging woman. I also heard stories of him being wronged by various people in town.

But, I was blissfully caught up in the romance of the relationship and shrugged off and rationalized every single one of these things.

The thing is, assholes are the most amazing lovers (am I not right?) - especially in the beginning. When they determine to pursue you, win you and love-bomb you, it feels like the kind of love you only read about in romance novels – an intoxicating, soaring "you and me against the world," I've never been this happy, you are my one true soulmate kind of love. It's easy to rationalize away the "What the f" moments.

We're swept off our feet, and become totally caught up in the hope, energy and excitement of a future with this perfect person we've found - two people vibrating at a crazy high frequency, completely in-sync and wildly attracted to each other. And we *never* forget that feeling. Read that again: *We. Never. Forget. That. Feeling.* We later will come to desperately crave those highs when they aren't there.

Eventually, when (note keyword: "*when*") our prince charming or princess inevitably reveals their asshole selves to us (assholes always do), here's what we good empaths do like clockwork:

--- we rationalize the bad behavior
--- we ignore
--- we white-wash
... and, we attempt to fix.

I guarantee if you're involved with an asshole right now, you are adept at one (or all) of the above.

We empaths not only create excuses for our assholes' bad behavior, we (*gasp*) imagine it's *us* who must somehow partly (or largely) be to blame for our partner's mistakes or loss of temper. We convince ourselves if *we* just try harder we can help them be better humans. After all, we want to get back to those highs we love so much (those pleasure-full eyes-rolled-back-in-the head love-bombing moments). They obviously need us to bring out their loving side and we're here for them.

When the inevitable "bad times" come, when we are subjected to their wretched behavior and finally express horror and displeasure or concern, sometimes even *they too* realize how awful they're being. They shift gears and revert back to the sweet, loving, affectionate, romantic lover we so miss. It's kisses and hugs and tenderness, and "I love you madly" and we're back smack dab in the middle of the honeymoon phase again.

And we're happy for the moment to return, but sadly we're sucked back into the vortex of an unhealthy relationship, left only to wonder when our person will get angry again or a new drama will pop up (we always naively hope it will be never but it always does). There might be long periods of time that will pass during which they will be "good" until they're "bad" again. And the cycle repeats.

In my case, I viewed it as my new job to keep my sweet guy happy and avoid anything that would cause him to get angry with *me.* I saw his anger towards other people, and at times it truly scared me. There were road rage incidents. And there were times he talked of shooting people he was angry with. There were lots of guns around him. I never questioned why, though. I was just determined he would never be angry like that with me. I would be his "safe" place.

And most of the time he wasn't ever angry with me. He treated me wonderfully and was always charming in the beginning. We quickly began to spend all of our time with each other. My friends tell me now they noticed they didn't see me anymore. My weekly dinners with them went away. And my parents also say they never saw me much anymore – another later-to-be–learned textbook warning sign that I was falling into an unhealthy relationship.

There were certain people I learned that I should not associate with and I also learned not to invite certain people to be guests on my radio show. These were people he had had fallings-out with. Like any loyal partner, I needed to steer clear of those people. I did so, gladly, as I was completely loyal to him.

Meanwhile, I determined my job in life was to make him happy and give him everything he wanted at all times. I indulged him in every way. We had massage tables in every house. Whenever he wanted a foot massage or a 60-90 minute full body massage he got it (even if it was at night and I was tired). If he wanted chocolate chip cookies late in the evening, I baked him chocolate chip cookies. There wasn't anything I wouldn't do for him, or give him. My world centered on pleasing him and making sure he stayed happy. I loved him. He was my world.

Then, gradually I felt the control ramp up. He wanted me to wear only black bras and panties. I couldn't wear perfume or high heels. He didn't like me to wear nail polish (on my toes was okay, but not on my fingernails). And, no jewelry. And behind closed doors, to my shock, I started to experience his anger directed at me, too.

He would get angry with me for preparing too much food at dinner time or for deciding we should host a dinner party – he told me he really hated dinner parties as we waited for a house full of guests to arrive to our house. I would get in trouble for feeding the barn animals too much, and for buying too much hay (even though I was paying for everything). I always walked on eggshells around him, never knowing what would set him off.

Welcome to: "Crazy-making"

What I didn't know back then was the very first "What the…?" moment I experienced and all those "What the…?" moments that followed were the early stage in this thing called "crazy-making" that happens in narcissistic relationships.

There are three stages to crazy making, and only in retrospect can we clearly see how we fell into it and how it would soon become part of what is known as the "cycle of abuse."

Crazy-making defined:
Crazy-making: behavior that on the surface appears to be about one thing but underneath is about something entirely different and is about manipulating and controlling you. Crazy-making is abusive behavior intended to deflate and reduce you to change your behavior and throw you off-center emotionally. In the end, the crazy-making makes you easier to control as you question yourself. It is behavior that is not logical, does not make sense and is not based on truth. You're put in a "can't win"

situation.

The stages of crazy-making:

Stage 1:

Confusion. You can't quite grasp what's happening.

"What did he say?"

"Why did he say that?"

"Why would he do that?"

Stage 2:

You begin to make excuses for him and defend him.

"Maybe he's tired."

"He does like things done a certain way."

"He's so loving other times."

Stage 3:

You begin to question yourself, blaming yourself. Warning: This is the stage where you begin to lose your sense of self.

"Maybe it is my fault."

"I was being unreasonable."

"I was wrong."

"Maybe there is something wrong with me."

There are three things to know about narcissists:

1. **Narcissists begin relationships as loving, wonderful charming people.** And, they *are* wonderful and charming people in the beginning. They *do* love you. They aren't stupid people. They are

often highly intelligent people and they know a good thing when they have it, but (wait for it)...

2. **They change**. All relationships with narcissists change. All prince charmings and princesses who are narcissists change. Once you're hooked, they turn into assholes. They fundamentally cannot sustain living at a healthy high positive frequency for long and are highly susceptible to unhealthy influences (selfishness, control by family members, love of money, need for control, huge egos, etc.). They become a person you don't even recognize. You're left confused. How could things have gone so wrong? What happened??

3. **Sadly, if you don't get away, or have a major life reset with your asshole to fix the relationship, most relationships with assholes become abusive**. That's because all narcissists/assholes become abusive eventually. And so, identifying them (as early as possible) is all-important, and getting away from them and healing even more so.

And so, as you work hard to keep the peace and avoid more "What the..." moments, be aware you need to up your game if you're in deep with an asshole.

Worksheet #1

Have you experienced any "What the f... ?" moments?

Have you experienced crazy-making moments? List them here.

Chapter 3
Is He an Asshole?

S*o, is my person an asshole?...* you ask. You want to know for sure.

How do we distinguish between an ordinary person like you and me who only occasionally acts like an asshole and does dopey things and a bona fide run-for-the-hills asshole that this book is about?

The quick answer, although not scientific, most likely lies in how you answer this one question:

Do you *consistently* feel uncared for, not valued, confused, betrayed, and belittled by this person?

Honestly, it's as simple as the answer to that. Do you?

If the answer is yes, you consistently feel this way (... again, wait for it)... yep, chances are you're with an asshole.

But as a double-check if you like, solicit the help of your friends. Ask them if they see the same asshole behaviors you see.

"Is John an asshole?... What do you think?"

You might be relieved to learn that you're not the only one who's noticed something is off. Listen to their comments and opinions carefully. You're in information-gathering mode right now.

Wait, what if I'm the narcissist??.... am I the asshole here?

Most of us who are seeking answers have asked that question at some point. I asked the same question. It's textbook that we empaths ask that of ourselves.

If you're wrapped up with a narcissist right now and stopping to question and wonder if you're a narcissist, here's your answer:

First of all, narcissists do not have a conscience. You, on the other hand, being the empath that you are, have an overabundance of conscience and a governing sense of right and wrong that dictates how you believe everyone should behave.

Second, narcissists lack empathy. They are self-centered, selfish and have no sense of (or care about) pain they inflict on others. You care *too* much. That's why you're questioning even yourself if you're the asshole. Empaths take on and absorb the emotions of those around them, want to constantly please, and have a hard time saying no and setting boundaries.

The answer is, no. You're not the asshole. You're not the narcissist. The fact that you're an empath worrying and wondering if you're the narcissist is proof that you're not. So there.

Chapter 4
Red Flags

There was a time when I wouldn't have known a red flag if it had walked up and introduced itself. I didn't know what one was and why I should even be concerned about looking for them. I know now, spotting a narcissist has everything to do with recognizing red flags.

Fact: All assholes/narcissists exhibit the same early red flags and warning signs.

If (keyword: *if*) you recognize red flags early, you can save yourself a lot of heartache by not getting in too deep with your asshole/narcissist and you can bail out early. If you're already in deep with a narcissist, you can at least confirm what you're dealing with and decide how and if you should leave, or if there's even hope for your relationship.

Chances are, you're like me and were never taught about red flags or what to look for.

Here are some indicators that, yes, you've got an asshole by the tail. Not all assholes exhibit *all* of these warning signs. But all assholes show *some* of these warning signs:

Do any of these apply to your person?

Red Flags:

- ☐ All of their exes are crazy (by far, the most prevalent red flag)
- ☐ They always perceive and portray themselves as the "victim" in failed personal & business relationships
- ☐ They have anger issues
- ☐ Nothing is ever their fault
- ☐ They have a need to be in control
- ☐ They have a long history of run-ins with people
- ☐ They constantly change their mind, so much so that it's hard to keep up
- ☐ They love-bomb in the beginning of the relationship (may favorite part of life with a narcissist, but I digress)
- ☐ They want you to spend all your time with them, to the exclusion of your family and friends
- ☐ Their needs always come first
- ☐ They're financially slippery
- ☐ They are cruel to animals
- ☐ They gaslight you (deny things that are obvious, their actions don't match their words, tell you you're wrong, you're too sensitive, crazy, or all the above)
- ☐ They get angry at the suggestion they could be wrong
- ☐ They alternate between mean and sweet
- ☐ They accuse you of doing things you're not doing
- ☐ They give you the silent treatment as punishment when angry

- ☐ They never make you feel secure and safe
- ☐ You find yourself constantly walking on eggshells around them
- ☐ They're overconfident
- ☐ They blame others for their behavior and poor decisions
- ☐ They take pleasure in sabotaging and ruining special occasions to create drama and bring the focus on themselves
- ☐ They belittle you with words and actions
- ☐ They act childish when they don't get their way
- ☐ They control how you dress
- ☐ They never apologize
- ☐ They have a history of appearing intoxicated in public, and show signs of possible addiction to alcohol or drugs
- ☐ They promise a great future but never deliver on promises

<u>Has your asshole ever said any of the following to you?</u>

"I never said that."
"Stop being so sensitive."
"You're crazy."
"You didn't hear me right."
"Can't you take a joke?"
"There you go again."
"I wouldn't do (this), if you didn't do (fill in the blank)."
"You're not remembering things correctly."

I'm the first to admit I ignored so many red flags. Maybe that's because we're conditioned in life to ignore red flags. The smoke alarm in my house has gone off in the middle of the night several times over the years alerting me to a fire. I always pull the battery and go back to bed. There's never been a fire. I take it as just another false alarm. No visible smoke. No fire.

I hear car alarms going off all the time and none of us panic. There's never a car burglary in progress. It's never anything to be alarmed about.

This is serious business, though. Red flags should be noted and noticed. They should be recognized. It's important to recognize patterns in red flags.

When you recognize a pattern you can see things you didn't see before. You can understand things that are happening and you can anticipate things. You're ready. You're not thrown off center. Recognizing red flags allows you, in the middle of all the noise, to understand what all this means. That is immense power!

Worksheet #2

Have you noticed any red flags in your relationship? Note them here.

Worksheet #3

What are some things you're unhappy with in your relationship?

Worksheet #4

What are some things you're happy with in your relationship?

Chapter 5
Ask Yourself These Questions

Review these questions and check those that apply to you and your relationship (i.e. check the box if the answer to the question is "YES"):

- ☐ Have you begun to suspect that your relationship is unhealthy?
- ☐ Do you feel trapped and lonely?
- ☐ Do you ever feel your partner is hiding something from you or not honest about certain things?
- ☐ Do you try to express your feelings and needs to your partner, but your partner ignores you or becomes angry when you share your thoughts?
- ☐ Are you verbally abused?
- ☐ Are you ever physically abused (hit, punched, shoved, sexually assaulted)?
- ☐ Do you suppress your feelings/needs in the relationship in order to keep the peace?
- ☐ Do you secretly cry in private as your only release of sadness and frustration having to do with your relationship?

- ☐ Do you find yourself spending a lot of time hoping that your partner will change?
- ☐ Do you wonder why your partner does certain things if they love you?
- ☐ Do you feel physically and emotionally exhausted trying to constantly please your partner or communicate in a healthy manner?
- ☐ Do you tell yourself, "… if only I try harder and do better, he won't get to this point again"…?
- ☐ Do you worry that this is your last chance for love and you'd better do everything you can to make it work?
- ☐ Has your partner given you an STD?
- ☐ Has your partner ever drugged you?
- ☐ Does your partner stay out all night?
- ☐ Has your partner cheated on you?
- ☐ Has your partner ever been violent with you?
- ☐ Does your partner punish you when they're angry?
- ☐ Are you ever afraid of your partner?

Let's be honest, now. Be real. How many of these apply to you?

Do any of them sound like *your* situation?

If so, it's time to get serious about getting healthy and breaking free from a toxic relationship that is destined to become abusive if it isn't already.

I'm so sorry sweet thing, you're with an asshole.

If the answer to one or more of these questions above is "YES"—get ready to walk away.

Chapter 6
Let's Talk About Abuse

Let's talk about domestic abuse. It's too important a topic to not address head on.

It hurts my heart to know how many millions of women (and in some cases, men) are hurt physically and emotionally each year. Lives are shattered as these sweet souls are preyed upon. Domestic abuse is truly traumatizing. And far too often, victims are surprised to learn what they experience is legally defined as domestic abuse and domestic violence, so let's talk about it here.

Domestic abuse and domestic violence, in fact, are terms that largely describe identical conduct. Depending on where you live, the legal definitions may vary.

The National Coalition Against Domestic Violence defines domestic violence as "willful intimidation as part of a systemic pattern of power and control perpetrated by one intimate partner against another. Frequency and severity of domestic violence can vary dramatically, but the constant of domestic violence is one partner's consistent efforts to maintain power and control over the other."

Another victim advocacy group, The National Domestic Violence Hotline, defines domestic violence as follows: "Domestic violence (also called intimate partner violence (IPV), domestic abuse or relationship abuse) is a pattern of behaviors used by one partner to maintain power and control over another partner in an intimate relationship."

Domestic abuse affects women and men across all spectrums of age, race, socioeconomic level and nationalities.

The U.S. Department of Justice states that 1 in 4 women and 1 in 9 men at some time experience "severe intimate partner physical violence, intimate partner sexual violence, and/or intimate partner stalking with impacts such as injury, fearfulness, PTSD, use of victim services, etc."

(Source: https://www.bjs.gov/content/pub/pdf/ndv0312.pdf)

Domestic abuse also takes on forms besides physical abuse and sexual abuse. Other forms of domestic abuse include:

- psychological abuse
- financial abuse (extremely common, but perhaps the least obvious form of abuse)
- reproductive coercion (gaining more attention in recent years)

I've learned people are very uncomfortable with discussing domestic abuse. They want to turn a blind eye to it. What they don't realize is speaking out about it and raising awareness is the only way to break the cycle of abuse and help victims heal. Abuse thrives in secrecy. And, secrecy thrives when abusers bully and shame victims into silence. Fear of retaliation and fear of embarrassment and ridicule should never keep a victim silent.

If you are suffering at the hands of abuse, listen carefully. Tell someone. Please tell someone what you're going through. Don't remain paralyzed in fear. There are many of us who love you and understand and want to help you.

Maybe, you're just now realizing you are in an abusive situation and you're disheartened that you didn't recognize the red flags. Don't shame yourself. It's extremely difficult to tell early on in a relationship if it will become abusive. It takes time and distance to see a pattern, especially because of the trauma bonding you're experiencing (more on that later).

It's important now you educate yourself now on the textbook patterns of abuse. Make no mistake, there is a distinct pattern – distinct stages – to the cycle of abuse that almost all abusers follow.

Chapter 7
Textbook Patterns

Here are the five stages of narcissistic abuse. Study them here so you recognize the cycle.

The Cycle of Narcissistic Abuse

Stage #1
Love-bombing

First, comes the love-bombing and idealization stage.

This is where you are showered with adoration and attention. You're swept off your feet by the care and affection shown by your narcissist, you're full of hope, joyous and the relationship develops quickly with effortless ease.

At this stage, the abuser charms his/her victim, gaining their trust, saying what they believe the target wants to hear, and showing incredible tenderness. Both parties openly and lovingly give of themselves and fall completely in love. You are treated the way you always dreamed of being treated. He adores you. You're his soulmate, his prize, his angel. He tells you he's never been happier in his life. You are soulmates.

Then, once you are committed to the relationship, the relationship will begin to change. You're slowly isolated away from friends and family.

And the control ramps up and the abuse begins. Again, the abuse can take many forms: physical, emotional, social, financial, and more. They will begin to control your finances, your career, social outings, who you see, what you do. This leads to tension-building.

Stage #2
Tension building

Tensions begin to rise and the victim begins to see another side to the abuser. The abused begins to "walk on eggshells" around the narcissist, fearing his/her moods, and focusing on placating him/her.

Stage #3
Abusive behavior

An incident happens where the abuser does something that hurts the victim (emotionally, physically, financially, etc.). He is controlling and intimidating. Usually one or more tactic is used.

Stage #4
Victim reacts

After the incident, the abused reacts and shows displeasure or fights back in some way. One of two things then happen. The abuser apologizes for the incident and makes promises to be better in the future and the relationship moves to reconciliation. Or, the abuser shockingly blames the victim for the incident or accuses them of being crazy or too sensitive, or completely dismisses the bad behavior as "not that bad." The abused then retreats, submits and internalizes what happens.

Either way, the victim (whether she realizes it or not) submits to the reality of abuse being a part of the relationship and begins to question whether she caused the problem. She accepts the apology and pledges within her own mind to try harder ("*If I just try harder, this won't happen again.*). The victim is sucked yet again back into the relationship. All this is followed by another smooth happy "honeymoon phase."

Stage #5
Reconciliation/calm

This is a period of normalization that unfortunately emboldens the abuser that all is once again good and reassures him that he is empowered and there is no threat to his authority. The cycle of placating the asshole to keep the peace then begins again.

Each phase may last different lengths of time, with the honeymoon phase sometimes being a good length of time and being the carrot that the victim is always reaching for, to get back to. The victim wants the kinds words, the affection, the loving partner back, the love-bombing. They crave the adoration and the sex, tender and passionate. And they do get it when they threaten to leave. Again, textbook.

All the while during the abuse these women try hard to maintain a sense of normalcy to outsiders that all is okay in the relationship. That is, until some event occurs to where they no longer can.

And so, the asshole becomes the center of the victim's world. We continue running on the hamster wheel of constantly trying to measure up and please them.

Final Stage
Devaluation & Discard

Eventually, when the abuse goes too far and the relationship inevitably breaks down, the "devaluation & discard" phase begins. This is often the most difficult stage for victims. When you no longer serve the narcissist's purpose and can no longer be controlled, they find new narcissistic supply elsewhere (they always do, again, textbook) and you are discarded.

You come to realize he was never truly in love with you. True love cannot be turned on and off so quickly. He changed and was only in love with what you could do for him. Maybe he didn't want to be alone. Maybe you satisfied his ego. Maybe you helped him appear stable and respectable. But in the end, he was only in love with what you could do for him. In some cases, he was only interested in financially draining you of all resources.

The abuser will then use all tactics available for warfare against you: gas-lighting, triangulation, smearing your name and reputation, flying monkeys, and more.

No one who escapes from an abuser does so cleanly. Often, they are stalked and harassed even years later by the asshole and more often, by their flying monkeys. Again, flying monkeys are friends, family and employees of abusers who are easily convinced to harass and intimidate the abused on the abuser's behalf (abuse by proxy, if you will). You *will* experience flying monkeys if you're trying to escape from a raging narcissist (again, textbook).

Assholes are vindictive. And victims are left emotionally destroyed, financially devastated, many suffering from depression, anxiety attacks, and CPTSD (Complex Post Traumatic Stress Disorder). In extreme cases, some victims commit suicide or come close to it.

For women faced with the secret reality of abuse, it's hard for them to communicate the abuse to others when they're in it. They often feel isolated and lonely and trapped inside the abusive relationship and held hostage to the trauma bond created that keeps them going back.

What you may be surprised to learn about assholes

You may be surprised to learn that abusers and assholes aren't as strong and emotionally confident as you think. You may be surprised to learn that assholes are inherently insecure, even the handsome ones. They also have a chronic fear of abandonment. Their response is very angry when you leave them. It's important for them to always win at any cost to keep what they want.

Besides abandonment, one of their other big fears is growing old. Aging means loss of looks and declining finances. They pride themselves on presenting to the world an image of prestige and integrity, but these are hard to sustain long-term.

Narcissists also share many other characteristics:

- self-centeredness
- want to win at all costs
- present themselves as honorable with high morals
- have no conscience and no remorse
- are arrogant
- inflated sense of self
- lack empathy
- become angered when they are challenged
- more concerned about how things "look"
- fragile sense of esteem
- sense of entitlement (won't wait in lines, feel deserving of preferential treatment)
- excellent at creating confusion
- constantly blame others
- claim to be innocent in all respects
- are highly offended by the truth
- make sure abuse takes place behind closed doors

And we empaths all share similar characteristics, too:

- we blame ourselves

- we ignore red flags
- we all try to leave. The average victim tries to leave seven times during the course of an abusive relationship before finally escaping.

Chapter 8
If You're a Friend or Family Member

If you are a friend or family member of someone in a relationship with an asshole, you need to know there are some specific things you can do to help, and some things you should ***not*** do (if your aim is to, of course, cause no further harm).

You need to realize that the abuse started out slowly, in small gradual stages until your loved one was programmed to accept the bad behavior. They were slowly made to feel insignificant and unimportant and their needs and concerns ignored. They were the frog in the gradually heated pot of boiling water not knowing they were in trouble until it was too late.

It's also important to understand there's probably a 99% chance your loved one is an empath. And knowing about empaths will help you understand how they fell into this situation and how you can help them get out.

What is an empath?

We're people pleasers. We worry about other people's needs and happiness. We don't like to disappoint people. We are very much affected by the moods and emotions of people around us. We are doting, loyal and selfless to a fault. We love people. We love to help people. We are caregivers by nature.

Empaths are nurturing, highly sensitive, and extremely trusting. They will give of themselves to someone they love to the point of utter exhaustion and will strive to "keep the peace" at all times (assholes *love* this about us). We are affectionate, highly spiritual, and always put the needs of their partners first (again, narcs *love love love* this about us). When we love you, we will say "yes" a hundred times when we really want to say "no."

Yep, assholes are wildly attracted to us. And we empaths, to them. Ugh, the perfect storm.

And, just so you know when dealing with your empath, because of their extreme sensitivity, they dislike being rushed, arguing, loud noises, being in crowds, fake conversations, and inauthenticity. Because their needs often take a back seat, they often don't feel heard.

Healthy empaths, on the other hand, put their needs first and set clear boundaries in relationships. That's something to remember as you embark to help your loved one heal and get healthy.

Empaths are usually completely destroyed by toxic relationships that unravel, and are left feeling overwhelmed and full of sadness. They sink into hopelessness and sometimes severe depression. Many contemplate suicide because they just want the pain and abuse to end. It's an understatement to say they are extremely traumatized and confused when trying to leave and heal from an abusive situation. This is serious stuff.

Do *not* say the things most likely to roll off the lips of ignorant bystanders: "*Why don't you just leave?*" ... or, "*Why do you keep going back?*"... or, "*Just get over it, move on.*"

It's strange how quick people are to ask these questions rather than questioning WHY he abuses her in the first place... but, I digress.

In asking - "*Why don't you just leave? Why do you keep going back?*" – you're showing the depth to which you truly don't understand how badly the abuse has damaged her psyche.

Why does she keep going back? Why can't she just leave and move on?

There are four reasons why she has a hard time leaving and keeps going back to him:

Reason #1: because the relationship didn't start out as abusive.

She hopes and believes the abuser will change. She's ever hopeful. She's a healer, an empath.

She remembers that the relationship started out wonderful. She faithfully holds on to the positive aspects that exist in the relationship. After all, he was "good" and unbelievably loving for long periods of time after "bad" episodes. And when times are "good" they are truly over-the-top wonderful.

Here's what she's thinking to herself:

"Things will get better."

"He'll stop eventually. He loves me."

"The old him will come back."

"He didn't mean it."

"I'm not perfect either."

"No relationship is perfect."

"He needs me."

"He wouldn't hurt me intentionally. He's under stress."

Reason #2 why she keeps going back and has a hard time leaving: self-blame.

"I'm responsible for him acting like this."

"He loves me. Look at how I drove him do these things."

She perceives it as her failure to sustain the good relationship. And she doesn't want to discuss her failures with you. She doesn't want to be told to leave. She doesn't want to be rushed in making a decision to leave. She might not be ready to hear some of your advice. She just resolves to try harder.

An empath at heart, she focuses on healing the situation and giving even more. That's the solution in her mind. Everyone knows you have to give your all to make relationships work and that's what she's going to do.

Reason #3 why she keeps going back and has a hard time leaving: fear

There is tremendous fear of what will happen if she leaves because of dependency on the abuser… emotionally, socially, and financially. There is fear of his wrath for exposing abuse. There is fear of ridicule from friends. There is fear of being caught by the abuser discussing the abuse with anyone. The shame and fear makes her cower and want to hide.

And, to be honest, your abused loved one is fearful for very good reason!

Leaving is the single most dangerous time for victims of abuse.

The point where a victim begins to recognize abuse, makes objections, and discusses leaving, is the point when they become a threat to the abuser. That's the game-changer for the narcissist that ratchets up the abuse.

That's when threats are made. That's when the worst violence occurs. That's when flying monkeys are unleashed. That's when the abuser sets out to smear the victim with friends and associates. Your loved one is made out to be the abuser and the abuser acts the victim to get sympathy. They create smoke and mirrors to distract from the truth. That's when the abuser takes any and all steps to quickly silence the victim. It gets ugly, ugly, ugly.

It's your job to remind your loved one that their safety is everyone's primary concern and fear of embarrassment, shame, ridicule or judgment should never—ever— keep or make them silent. They need to tell someone, tell everyone what they're going through, and seek the help they need to be free from the asshole.

Reason #4 why she keeps going back and has a hard time leaving: she doesn't realize it's domestic abuse.

Learning about abuse, the cycle of abuse and the textbook behaviors helps you help them recognize with certainty when it's time to leave, in order to keep them safe. Learning about patterns of abuse helps break the trauma bond.

You would think that someone hurting you would break any bond or attachment you have with them. But in these cases, being hurt by someone that you deeply love – and being caught up in the cycle of abuse - creates a trauma bond that keeps her there.

So, don't mock and taunt women for going back or having a hard time leaving.It's part of the process of breaking free and healing.

Be compassionate. Don't re-victimize her. Don't abuse her further.

Don't say:

"I don't think he meant to hurt you."

"It can't be that bad, or you would leave."

"There are two sides to every story."

"Just get over it."

Do say:

"He seems to be hurting you a lot."

"I'm here for you if you want help. We will help you get out of this and heal."

"You are loved. We are here when you're ready to leave."

Ask her questions. Don't blame her. Recognize that her responses are very legitimate reactions to abuse, and tell her as much.

Here are some likely things your loved one is struggling with and how you can help:

--- **Victims need to feel safe to speak out and ask for help**. The abuse has thrived in secrecy and has made breaking free and healing difficult. They are often too afraid to come forward and share. Give your loved one a safe place to land. That's the most loving gift you can give her.

--- **Survivors are often gas-lighted by society** and by ignorant and misguided friends who dismiss the trauma. That re-traumatizes your loved one and makes them feel like they have no support. They are told that the abuser is a "nice guy," that this is just a bad breakup, get on with your life.

--- **Be sensitive to the fact that some victims struggle with PTSD (Post Traumatic Stress Disorder) and CPTSD (Complex Post Traumatic Stress Disorder)** which are psychological injuries caused by trauma. Sufferers struggle with panic attacks, nightmares, flashbacks, depression, fear and suicidal thoughts.

--- **And finally, take care not to collude with the asshole** in any way initiated by him/her or fall for their attempts to get you to turn your attention to the victim. Remember this: When you don't stand up for the victim, you are emboldening the abuser.

Chapter 9
On the Brink of Desperation – Triage Plan

No matter where you are in your journey right now, I can tell you I've been where you are. I've been at the falling in love stage, the love-bombing stage. I've had the first "What the..?" moments. I've tried to leave. I've gone back. I made excuses. I tried harder. I blamed myself. I experienced the fear. I also experienced the hopelessness, and the not-knowing-where-to-turn confusion.

Back then when I was struggling to just get by day to day, I wish I had known some survival tips for when things got crazy.

Is that where you are right now?

Feeling overwhelmed?

Desperate?

Edgy, nervous?

Having bouts of crying?

Do you feel like things are out of control and you're barely hanging on?

When everything is crazy and you feel completely hopeless, here's a TRIAGE PLAN to fall back on, as many times as you need to during your healing process. Just like hospital emergency rooms use triage plans to quickly stabilize patients who come through the door when in dire crisis, here's your own triage plan for dealing with your asshole.

TRIAGE PLAN

Note: Before you get started, I have to ask: Are you in danger? If so, call your local police department for help and advice in developing a safety plan.

Also, have you had any suicidal thoughts? If so, please stop everything and reach out to your nearest suicide crisis center. In the U.S., call the National Suicide Prevention Lifeline at 1-800-273-8255 (available 24 hours a day). If you're outside of the U.S., search Wikipedia online for their "List of suicide crisis lines" worldwide. You are precious and valued and there will be someone specialized in suicide prevention who can help you. Many women who leave toxic relationships contemplate suicide – even those who have never suffered from depression or contemplated suicide before. Even a simple "I am in so much pain, I don't want to wake up tomorrow" thought, is reason for you to reach out for help... immediately.

Back to the Triage Plan...

STEP #1:
TALK TO SOMEONE.

Seek out help from someone you trust... a friend, family member or co-worker. You need someone to talk to right now. Not tomorrow, or the next day, now. Talk to someone.

Tell them what you're feeling. Having the ear of a kind heart who can listen and share a different perspective and lend advice is invaluable right now. You need a loving support network around you. And, don't be discouraged if the first person you talk to isn't helpful. Don't stop until you find *someone* to open up to.

STEP #2:
PAUSE. MEDITATE. PERSEVERE.

Basically, slow down, breathe and focus on slowly and carefully taking baby steps forward. Don't react or don't make rash decisions. Don't lash out emotionally. Resist the temptation to (I know it's hard, but trust me on this one) lash out at your asshole.

Detach and rest in this moment. Your priority and focus right now is to center yourself and quiet the chaos in your mind. The best way to do that is to pray or meditate… whatever you want to call it. Even if only for 5 minutes, just do it.

And resolve to get through the day, repeating the breathing and meditating as many times as necessary.

STEP #3:
DO THINGS THAT MAKE YOU FEEL GOOD (SELF CARE)

Next, divert your attention away from the madness of your situation to something positive that simply makes you feel good: a hot Epson salt bath, staying in bed for a few hours with the covers pulled up over your head, a pedicure, binge-watching Netflix, a killer workout at the gym, a glass of wine with a friend, take a walk, write about how you feel, listen to music… just pick your pleasure and do it, girl! Whatever is good for your soul, do that!

This is your free pass right now to simply lean in and do what feels good! Focus on a favorite indulgence available right now and unwind. Your goal is self-care and to relax and make it through these difficult hours.

These three things will get you through the worst moments. Repeat them as many times as needed. Having this little bit of control and the ability to focus on positive things will give us a sense of peace.

And know this: Better days are coming! You can win this fight. You *will* win this fight!

TRIAGE PLAN RECAP:

STEP #1: TALK TO SOMEONE.

STEP #2: PAUSE. MEDITATE. PERSEVERE.

STEP #3: DO THINGS THAT MAKE YOU FEEL GOOD.

Worksheet #5
TRIAGE WORKSHEET

STEP #1: TALK TO SOMEONE.

Who are some people you can talk to? List them here.

STEP #2: PAUSE. MEDITATE. PERSEVERE.

Light a candle. Sit and breathe. Pray/meditate. Create a ritual to sit in calmness and regroup. What are some ways you can relax?

STEP #3: DO THINGS THAT MAKE YOU FEEL GOOD

List some favorite things-to-do that will make you happy and help you unwind:

Chapter 10
Uh-oh, he's an asshole, now what?

Okay, so I get it now, I'm with an asshole, now what do I do?

The first step is to look at your current situation and consider how much power and influence they wield over you:

- ☐ Are you just dating?
- ☐ Are you married to him?
- ☐ Are you living together?
- ☐ Do you have children together?
- ☐ How much financial control does he have over you?
- ☐ Do you work together?
- ☐ How long have you been together?
- ☐ What financial obligations do you share?

The answers to some of these questions will determine how easy it is to distance yourself from an asshole and run for the hills and never look back.

Also, another important thing to consider:
Does your partner have a history of abusing or harassing previous partners before you?

If there is any history of harassment or court battles with previous romantic partners, you will probably be in for the same as you start to untangle yourself from the relationship and plan to leave.

If you're lucky though, yours might be a somewhat casual long-distance relationship where it will be easy to distance yourself and easily break up. Chances are though, leaving will be more difficult if you are not financially strong or he has isolated you socially.

There are 7 ways to leave a toxic relationship, depending on your situation:

1. The ghosting breakup

   Ghosting is a breakup where you end the relationship suddenly, abruptly, without any explanation and cease all communication completely. You go radio-silent, get it? Gone, see ya'!

   After you ghost someone, you also ignore all future attempts by them to communicate. It's pretty harsh but perfectly acceptable when you are new to a relationship and are truly getting creeped out. Cut your losses and bail. Ghosting is *not* practical, obviously, for anyone living together or partners who have kids together.

   Ask yourself:

   ☐ Could you easily ghost your asshole?

   ☐ Do you live in the same city?

   ☐ Do you work together?

2. The "This isn't working, let's just be friends" breakup

   This mutual and friendly kind of breakup (I like to call it, a "break-off") is never an option with an asshole.

   So, let's move on…

3. The Band-aid breakup

   Swift and painful like stripping off a band-aid. This involves acting like everything is normal with your partner and then executing a carefully crafted escape plan suddenly and swiftly. It's your best option in many cases, but is extremely difficult (or impossible) to pull off if you're living together or married. It *is* an option if you're merely dating.

4. The Hindenburg breakup.

   There are two kinds of Hindenburg breakups: those involving attorneys and the court system and those not involving attorneys and the court-system.

   Do one of these four breakup types above register with you?

   You may be wondering if you can just try harder and make things work in your relationship. I love your optimism and can-do attitude and trying harder would make sense for normal relationships, but consider this:

WHY TRYING HARDER DOES NOT WORK WITH ASSHOLES:

1. You will simply be continuing the same cycle of tolerating bad behavior and poor results that have made your life miserable. You *will* have more heartache if you stay.

2. The only thing that might make your asshole wake up is painful consequences. Only then will they make attempts to change their behavior.

3. You can't make your partner want to get healthy. *They* have to want to get healthy on their own.

4. This is not the worst thing you've ever been through. Let's get you through this and move on!

Chapter 11
Deciding to Leave

It bears repeating again, leaving is the single most dangerous time for victims of narcissists. It turns out assholes don't much like rejection and you leaving them. The point where they feel they're losing control of you is when they ratchet up the abuse. It is often a very scary time. Almost ¾ of domestic violence murders in the U.S. happen after the victim leaves, not before.

When deciding to leave, the first thing you should look at is safety concerns:

- Does your asshole have a past of any violence or harassing partners in the past?
- Are there any court records indicating other former partners have ever been fearful of him?
- Does he own guns?
- Has he ever threatened violence against anyone he was angry with (no matter if he actually followed through)?

These are indications that you should be worried for your safety (and for the safety of your children if you're a parent). Consider consulting an attorney in these instances or contacting local law enforcement for help and advice.

Leaving is the first step in recovering from an abusive relationship. I won't lie to you. Things will get harder and scarier from here on out before they get better.

Follow this checklist before considering leaving:

- ☐ Create a safety net around you. Make a list of trusted people you can turn to (a friend, a parent, etc.) as well as places where you can safely stay.
- ☐ Start creating a careful exit plan with an eye towards safety. The most dangerous assholes may become aggressive. Don't ever take them on alone. Don't meet or discuss matters with their associates or family and friends. Your asshole will want to appear the victim and unfortunately might do everything he can to make you look bad (if he follows textbook patterns).
- ☐ Keep a journal of evidence including threats (dates, copies of emails, audio recordings) and photos of abuse. Document, document, document. And, keep all the evidence in a safe place.
- ☐ Report to the police any scary or concerning incidents from your asshole or other people.
- ☐ Install extra security measures at your house: security cameras, outside cameras, chains on doors, home alarm, etc.
- ☐ Make copies of car keys and house keys and keep the copies in a separate location.
- ☐ Make photocopies of all important documents and credit cards and keep the copies in a safe location.
- ☐ Go to the hospital if you have suffered any injuries.
- ☐ Install a GPS tracker app on your phone (and those of your chil-

dren) so that someone will always know where you are.

- [ ] Discuss a safety plan with your children.

- [ ] If needed, set money aside to be ready to leave when you need it. Many narcissists make you financially dependent on them for money. If you need to, plan and save. I know women who have had to open up accounts and start secretly squirreling money away months and years in advance to be able to leave.

- [ ] Acknowledge that this is all upsetting, but stay strong and steadfast in moving toward freedom and safety. Don't be hard on yourself. You are just one of many victims of this person.

- [ ] Try to stay calm. They will try to make you look irrational by leaving. Stay focused on protecting yourself. Focus on your freedom. Focus on your healing.

At this point you have to be willing for this relationship to end. Firm up your resolve. Don't fall for any more insincere promises of change if they come your way. He might promise you the moon but won't have any intention of following through. Be firm and clear. If it helps, script out what to say in advance ("I can't live like this anymore"… "We both need help, and I'm going to leave to get help now"… "Your anger problem makes it impossible to work on our problems right now"… "I want this to work, but I need to get healthy now" etc.). You need to stand your ground. Don't continue to assume it's up to you to figure out a solution to the abuse. It's not up to you to "try harder."

If you need and want the following things from a healthy relationship, just know you won't get them with your asshole right now:

- a healthy relationship
- long-term happiness
- true love

- honesty
- safety
- peace of mind.

Leaving is only the first step in recovering from an abusive relationship. Yes, things will get harder before they get better, and it will be a long road. Friends and family will not understand and may not be entirely helpful. You likely will be re-victimized by lawyers and the court system and possibly even domestic violence advocacy groups.

It's up to you to move forward with a plan and you can get started today.

Chapter 12
28-Day Reset Plan

"You can't be that kid standing at the top of the waterslide, overthinking it. You have to go down the chute."

Tina Fey

Yep, don't overthink where you are. Just know that you're on good solid ground for moving forward. You're going to get through this. Now is your opportunity to define a new path forward for you, and only you… not your asshole's desires of what you should be.

For the next 28 days commit yourself to the following daily self-care reset plan:

Every day, commit to focusing intently only on you and your greatest passions and your healing (and *not* your asshole). Of course, if you have children, your focus remains steady on them, too, as always (and pets, and continuing family life). But my point is, you're making an intentional effort to focus on this plan towards getting strong and healing.

This reset plan will help you make lasting changes in your life. We will start to de-program bad habits and re-learn truths you need to embrace.

Do this program for 28 days, and you will be on your way to ridding yourself of the toxicity you've been living with.

In broad overview brush strokes, here's how we're going to do it:

1. You need a support system
2. You need to learn more about narcissistic abuse
3. You need to focus on what you're passionate about & getting healthy

You're wounded now. When you have a physical wound, the first thing we always do is cleanse it. Purify it. Tend to it. Rest it. Then, give it time and space to heal. The same goes for you when you have an emotional injury or wound.

Cleanse. Purify. Rest. Give it time and space to heal. That's the basis of this 28-day reset plan.

Before we get started though, it's important for you to understand that breakups with abusive narcissists aren't easy. You will think it's not possible to feel any worse than you do at this moment. Well, you will, sweet girl, I just want you to know.

Once these men realize they have lost control and respect, they WILL lash out in one of many ways. Chances are he will have no hesitation in trying to damage your reputation. He will gaslight you and make every effort to make moving on difficult and long and protracted. He will set his flying monkey on you to harass and torment you. And true to the textbook behavior of these men, he will soon replace you with a new narcissistic supply (someone who believes the image he projects of being honorable and charming, and provides him with the admiration he requires) in an attempt to show you how "replaceable" you are. Poof, just like that, the narcissist will be in love with someone new. Don't be surprised or upset. Make no mistake, this woman is being used. This is what these narcissists do. Again, textbook. It's all a reflection on them, and not you.

There will be days when missing him will feel like an unbearable heavy weight on your heart. The pain will ebb and flow.

But there will also be days when you realize you're better off without him. You will be begin to breathe deeply again. You'll know you're finally free and the pain of missing him will become more of a twinge rather than a constant dull ache.

It will be a roller coaster ride of emotions over the next 28 days. That's normal. I've been there.

It's important for you to remember, "there is no victory without a struggle!" So, embrace the struggle because you're after the sweet prize of freedom.

Just remember:

Purify.
Rest.
Give yourself time and space to heal.

And so, these first 28 days are critical to your healing. The focus is on getting you strong physically, mentally, spiritually in baby steps, since you're in a weakened state right now. You need structure and direction. This will give you a chance to reevaluate how you live, what you're doing and where you want to go next.

Ready?

Grab a notebook to take notes as you go, keeping a page for each day. Review the list every morning and several times throughout the day. Stay on track. Start implementing this plan immediately, one day at a time. Off you go, love!

28-DAY RESET PLAN

1. **Go "No Contact"**

   And no exceptions, girlfriend.

   "No Contact" means cutting off all communication with your asshole, completely no contact. No phone calls, no texts, no emails, no checking his Facebook and Instagram account, no talking to his friends, no nothing. "No Contact" means no going over to see him, no "bumping in to him," no sex, no seeing him in any conceivable way. Detoxing and detaching from your asshole is critical at this stage in your healing.

   Going "no contact" is very hard. The letting go part is extremely hard, I know. You will question if you've made a mistake and he's not an asshole. You will want him back. You will want to feel the good times again, and overlook the bad times.

   NOTE: NO CONTACT for 28 days is trickier when you have children together. In that case, all contact during the 28-day period should ONLY be concerning the children and nothing else. As much as you can, separate yourself from the asshole and fashion a plan that comes as close as possible to this 28-day reset plan. Protect the children and put their care and safety first, always.

2. **Surround yourself with a great support system.**

   You need to reconnect with those people the asshole wanted to distance you from – your family members and friends. The people you were separated from are the very people you need right now and who can help you.

   Quietly reach out to those people and break the social exile you've been under. Restore those relationships, reconnect, and develop a plan to see these loved ones and talk. If you haven't shared the truth of what you have been living, tell them what you're experiencing.

Out of this inner circle of trusted friends and family, select one person to be your mentor and accountability partner for the next 28 days. This person should be supportive and loving and agreeable to checking in with you every day to encourage you but not listen or tolerate your BS when you start back sliding. Their job is to make sure you stay on target with successfully completing the plan. Fill them in on the 28-Day Reset Plan. This person should NOT be an employee of yours, by the way.

Who are the people around you who can be your support team?

Who is your mentor/accountability partner?

3. **Pamper yourself every day.**

Self-care is an all-important part of healing when you're in your current state of feeling overwhelmed and hopeless.

How do you like to be pampered?

Face masks, hot baths, massages, yoga?

There are lots of ways to dote on yourself. Pick activities you love and do at least one of them daily for 28 days in a row!

Mix it up and do something different every day. Or, do the same thing every day. Make it be anything you're passionate about. Hobbies can also be a fun way to pamper yourself, if you have been denying yourself time devoted to enjoying them.

Need ideas? What about…

- aromatherapy
- buy yourself flowers
- spend time outside in nature (it's emotionally grounding)
- paint, cook, write poetry
- knit, play music, sing
- binge watch your favorite series on Netflix or Hulu
- read
- light candles
- workout
- or, simply be in the moment and have a cup of coffee at your favorite coffee shop, sitting alone for an hour to simply drink your coffee. Don't check your phone, or social media. Relax, sit, observe, enjoy the simple pleasure of just having a good cup of coffee.

Whatever is good for your soul and makes you feel pampered, do that.

How do you want to pamper yourself?

4. **Surround yourself with positive affirmations.**

   If you don't know what affirmations are, let's start there. They are simple positive thoughts and statements that we repeat to ourselves over and over again. What happens is our subconscious mind takes these in and programs them into our mind and thought reflexes.

   Write them on post-it notes and place them around the house where you see them multiple times a day: on your bathroom mirror, on your wall, on the desktop of your computer, on the background of your phone... everywhere. Commit to having a mindset of positivity and gratitude as you move forward.

   Here's my current list of affirmations:

   I am happy.
   I am healthy.
   I am strong.
   I am confident.
   I choose to see the goodness in all people.
   I welcome miracles in my life.
   I rejoice at the miracles that happen in my life.
   I greet each day with hope and enthusiasm.
   Everything in my life is working out for my highest good.
   I attract positive vibrations in my life.
   I attract uplifting and positive people in my life.
   I am at peace.
   I am divinely guided.
   I am protected and safe.
   I am loved.
   I am making a positive difference in the lives of other people.
   I completely and profoundly love and accept myself.
   I am powerful and vibrate at a high frequency.
   I release all negative thoughts and emotions that I experience.

I release all worries about the future.
I experience love wherever I go.
I am centered and at peace and nothing has the power to affect my peace of mind.
I am grateful for all the many blessings in my life.
I trust my intuition completely.
I see beauty in everything and everyone.
My home and surroundings are calming and nurturing to my soul.
I forgive everyone in my past & release with love all bad memories of things they've done.
I forgive my flying monkeys.
I send love to my flying monkeys.
I wish blessings for my flying monkeys.
I release all negativity in my life.
I embrace positivity.
Love flows throughout my body & my body heals itself continually and completely.
Everything I have buried deep in my psyche I release completely and let it all go.
I release all anger that I have unwittingly held on to.
I have a valuable purpose in this world.
I open my heart and accept love from all people around me.
I am grateful for all the love in my life.
I release all resentment, grief and trauma in my life.
I'm committed to giving my all in every one of my endeavors even up to the very end.
I choose love always.

5. **Start a bucket list.**

Have fun over the course of the next 28 days brainstorming 50 things you want to do or see before you die. This is will get you thinking about the future and things you want to do and accomplish, as opposed to what your asshole wants you to do. At the end of the month you will have your fun list to look forward to!

6. **Commit to exercising & eating healthy.**

   Say no to processed foods and make healthier meal choices. Exercise daily. And get at least eight hours of sleep every night. Make health & fitness a priority in your life for the next 28 days. Investing the time and effort in these areas will make you feel strong and sexy as you start the healing process. Besides, if you don't have energy or aren't in top form, nothing else good will follow.

7. **Meditate daily.**

   Your life is full of angst and chaos right now. Ground yourself every day for at least 5 minutes and you will begin to experience the peace and centeredness that only meditation can bring. If you're new to meditation, try a free guided app like Headspace or Calm.

8. **Allow yourself the freedom to grieve.**

   Be kind to yourself. Stop avoiding what you feel. Allow yourself to reflect and express your feelings in an outward way. Talk. Write. Cry. Share.

   You have been forced to suppress your feelings up to now. Whenever anyone is forced to suppress their feelings, they're made to feel insignificant and worthless. You are not insignificant. You are not worthless. As you have learned, suppressing feelings doesn't make them go away. It's damaging and hurtful. The only way to heal is to feel the pain and other sources of discomfort. Choose to do the work of processing your feelings.

   And protect your heart. Don't allow your peace of mind to be affected by the ridiculous actions of flying monkeys, for instance.

They don't control you or your emotions. Pity them.

9. **Protect your energy and time… by saying no!**

It's perfectly okay to say no, especially to people and things that don't support your healing and growth. As a recovering empath, you need to hear this loud and clear. It's okay to make choices that make YOU happy. It's okay to say "no" to being around people who are toxic and draining. It's okay to turn down invitations and instead choose to stay home alone. It's okay to let a phone call go to voice mail. It's okay to say you can't help. It's okay to say you're not available.

Say no at least once a day!

If you're uncomfortable saying no, practice with the following suggestions:

"Thank you for asking but I'm unable to."

"I would like to but I can't. I will let you know if something changes."

"I can't but I am able to do (this) for you."

"I realize you need my help, but I can't right now."

Honor your path. Don't be doormat. Stop saying "yes" out of obligation or guilt, and fear of disappointing people. This only results in built up resentment towards others and ourselves for not being able to say "no."

In the future, when you feel the urge to say no to people or requests, follow your gut and do it! Make that choice. No, no, no, no, no, no, no, glorious no!

10. **Start learning about abuse recovery.**

Explore on YouTube how others have struggled and healed. Read books, watch videos, listen to podcasts, visit your local library to see what other resources are available (audio books, e-books, seminars, etc.) on the topic of abuse recovery and self-improvement.

Now would be a good time to start seeing a counselor or therapist, if you haven't already - anyone who can give you clear and objective advice and help you deprogram from the lies you've been led to believe. Find one well-versed in trauma and abuse recovery.

Connect with a support group of women. As you listen to the stories of others, you will be amazed and encouraged by how many other women have experienced and felt what you're feeling. Learn as much as you can about self-improvement topics that interest you.

And, don't date until you're ready. Not that you likely will want to. In the same way that abusers are known to immediately replace their partners and find a new supply, victims won't want to get involved. The worse the abuse, the longer it will take for victims to be open to dating again. Abusers always quickly move on. Victims don't.

When it comes to dating, take your time and heal, instead. Honor this time of growth and healing and just have fun.

28 Day Reset Plan Daily Checklist

- ☐ Go NO CONTACT.
- ☐ Surround yourself with a great support system. Check in with your accountability partner daily.
- ☐ Pamper yourself every day.
- ☐ Surround yourself with positive affirmations.
- ☐ Start a bucket list.

- [ ] Commit to exercising and eating healthy.
- [ ] Meditate daily
- [ ] Allow yourself the freedom to grieve.
- [ ] Protect your energy and time… by saying no!
- [ ] Start learning more about abuse recovery.

Use the following daily sheets to track your thoughts and progress over the course of the next 28 days:

DAY 1

DAY 2

DAY 3

DAY 4

DAY 5

DAY 6

DAY 7

DAY 8

DAY 9

DAY 10

DAY 11

DAY 12

DAY 13

DAY 14

DAY 15

DAY 16

DAY 17

DAY 18

DAY 19

DAY 20

DAY 21

DAY 22

DAY 23

DAY 24

DAY 25

DAY 26

DAY 27

DAY 28

Worksheet #6

During your 28-day Reset Plan take time for introspection by answering the following questions:

Things I need to stop doing to improve my life:

Things I need to start doing to improve my life:

I am happiest when ________________________.

Dreams and goals I have:

Things I've done that I'm proud of:

The happiest time of my life was:

Boundaries I need to set:

Physical activities I love:

Hobbies & activities that give me joy:

Worksheet #7
My bucket list!

Chapter 13
How to Deal with an Asshole and Keep Your Sanity

Now that you know what you're dealing with, accept that the asshole is what he is. He may not always have been one, but he is now. And for the time being he isn't capable of loving you with any authentic deep connection. Right now, you're a possession to him. You benefited him and he loved you for what you could do for him. That's the most painful thing to realize and accept. But this is what will set you free... he never truly loved you with an honest long-lasting love. You were his supply – his primary narcissistic supply for a while – but you will be discarded and replaced, and replaced quickly. Someone else will become his primary supply now that you have outlived your usefulness.

In the meantime, some tips and tricks will prove helpful in how to deal with your asshole and keep your sanity.

1. Don't take any of this personally. It's not personal and never was. You truly are just a pawn in the game of life right now. There is nothing inherently wrong with you.

2. Don't doubt yourself and your perceptions. When the asshole employs mind-games and gas-lighting, and tactics of psychological control and power plays, don't fall for it.

3. Stick to firm boundaries with the asshole. Create as much space between them and you as possible (physically and emotionally). Make sure your "no" is a "no" and your "yes" is a "yes." Set boundaries and stick to them. Don't let them be manipulative and push the boundaries.

4. Let their games roll off your back. When they employ flying monkeys to carry on games for them, as much as possible look upon that misbehaving for what it is, too.

5. Document every type of abuse and aggression from your asshole. Keep a notebook with you at all times for that purpose.

6. Stop doing things to help your asshole. If they want help, they can help themselves. You are not their mother nor are you responsible for their health or wellbeing. And you're certainly not singularly responsible for the relationship. You are only responsible for you.

7. After your asshole has moved on, you may be hurt because they appear to move on quickly and are happy. Poof, just like that, the asshole is in love with someone new. There are a few things to know about the asshole after he moves on. The only thing new is their new supply. Nothing else has changed. Same manipulations, same need for control, same abuse, and the same love-bombing you were the target of (that part hurts). Have pity for the new supply. It may take her years, as it did you, to get away.

Here are some additional tips for communicating with your asshole that could keep him at bay. Of course, this is hard at times, since you're tired of his BS, but it's just to make your life easier. Be measured in how you respond to him.

When faced with a conversation that is heading nowhere good, try:

"I'm so sorry you feel that way. I suppose I just have to accept that's how you feel."

"I can't control how you feel, but I see you're upset."

When you want to conclude a conversation on your own terms try:

"It seems our views vary.... Let's agree to disagree and be done with it."

"I see you're upset. I'm going to go run some errands and when you're calmed down, I'll come back and we can talk more."

"Your opinions are really interesting. Let me think about them and get back to you."

I'm not suggesting you permanently suppress your feelings of outrage or whatever else you're feeling when dealing with your asshole. Find another time and place to release your frustrations. Cry, scream, write, just not in front of your asshole. If we don't get it out, we get drawn into ruminating on it and it chips away at our energy. And when you dwell on it all, they still control us.

Chapter 14
Is There Hope for My Asshole?

If you've gotten to this chapter and you're struggling and wondering, "*Is there hope for my asshole?*" and if you're torturing yourself with the following second thoughts, rest assured you're not alone:

- *I know I should leave my asshole, but...*
- *Maybe I should give him another chance...*
- *What if he changes for the better?*
- *My asshole isn't that bad...*
- *I still love him...*
- *He doesn't hit me or punch me, so...*

It's normal and actually quite admirable of you to optimistically hope for them to change. It's okay to question the decisions we carefully make each step of the way. Assholes are the hardest people to leave.

The answer to your question, "*Is there hope for my asshole?*" is sadly this: the older they are the more difficult it is for positive change. It takes an emotionally intelligent and intellectually strong man to do the hard work required, and sadly they are not emotionally intelligent and intellectually strong.

For most of them, it's difficult to change or to even want to change. Most narcissists never heal, in fact. They aren't willing to look at themselves and acknowledge their own accountability. They never go beyond a mere superficial relationship. And, they never have a desire to do the true spiritual work required. Worse, as they age and lose their looks and charm and realize they don't have what they want in the end, they become angry and depressed. They get worse over time.

There is one, and only one way there is hope for an asshole. I will preface by saying, however, I've never heard of any actual instances of it happening from the experts and thousands of recovering women I have spoken with. I compare it to the possibility of someone like you or I flying to the moon in a spaceship together. Theoretically, yes, it's *possible*, but...

If you're curious as to what that hope for an asshole looks like, I'll explain:

First, you would need to leave and restore yourself fully to alignment and high frequency with little concern about whether he does the same. You need to do the 11 step plan outlined in this book to get strong, to heal and be restored emotionally, spiritually, physically, and mentally. Here's the catch: Your asshole will need to do the same.

By the way, "*What is alignment?*" you ask.

Alignment is grounding yourself in love. Stay tuned, we will do a deep dive into a more thorough explanation of what being in alignment means and how to get in alignment (and stay there). Suffice it for now to know your asshole will need to do all the work required to "ground himself in love." If he does, there is hope. *If* he takes the same path to healing that you take, there is hope for the two of you. Again, it's extremely rare that this ever happens, but it is possible.

But it's important that all this work must be done individually. You can hope your asshole will do the same work you do, but you have no control over whether he does. If he does, and if he gets to the point where he is vibrating at a higher frequency and is back in alignment, and you both have the same vibrational high frequency, then you will be attracted to each other again. A true happy ending is possible. I've never actually seen this to happen in action for anyone (as I've mentioned, the narcissists never want to do the work), but theoretically it's possible.

It's also important to add if you go down this road, it's important that you get to the point where you are happy and strong and energetic on your own, without him. He cannot be your "goal" or reason for happiness. You have to feel good on your own and get to a point where you have an indifference as to whether he gets healthy or not.

Now, I am ever the optimist, hopeful that a happy ending can come with all assholes. To that end, if you are early in your relationship, here are some things you can do that may affect positive change early on, so there is stronger hope.

Here are four things you can do to strengthen your relationship:

1. Exercise "deep listening." Listen with a loving and attentive spirit with the intent to allow your asshole to say everything he wants to say. This is his opportunity to say everything on his little black heart, and you will listen. Deep listening between two people who are united in both wanting to build a stronger relationship is a good thing.

2. Be friendly and polite to your asshole. Don't react to their attempts to push your buttons. This might be the hardest thing ever, but it is not impossible.

3. Talk about "next steps."

4. Work together to set a realistic plan of how you will both work on the relationship.

In the meantime, stop apologizing for hoping for a storybook ending. Be confident. Develop an "*I don't care*" attitude if things don't go well.

Be yourself. Be fearless. Embrace everything that makes you beautifully you. Your imperfections. Your idiosyncrasies. No one is you. Focus on you and your healing.

Chapter 15
Missing Your Asshole

One of the most difficult things to do in life is remove someone from your heart. If you're like me, when you love someone, you love them forever.

It's painful to get over narcissists because you truly loved them with all your heart and were invested completely and honestly and authentically. Unfortunately, they were not. They have nothing to get over. You will be horrified by how fast you are replaced almost immediately and they skip away from the relationship seemingly un-phased and carefree. They are not invested. It always takes the victims much longer to heal.

I still miss my asshole. I miss him whispering in the back of my neck in bed, "Back in here," as he snuggled with me under the covers late at night. I miss the cute way every morning he would take off his boxer shorts and flip them up from the floor with his toes, in one sweeping motion. I miss how he showed me off to all his friends and made sure they knew how happy we were. I miss how he called and texted throughout the day every day.

Do I want him back now? No. I want a partner who is spiritually strong and working hard to stay aligned like I am. And, despite missing all these things I mentioned, I remember the bad. I deserve so much better than what he put me through. No woman deserves what he did to me. I deserve true and healthy love in my life. I deserve peace. You deserve true and healthy love, too. And, peace.

Let's do a reality check, sweet girl. This con artist (and yes, he's a con artist) has hurt you, demeaned you and stolen your light and clarity from you. He's left you feeling hopeless and defeated. You were a pawn in his life to satisfy his needs. You know all of that and yet you still miss him.

I don't mean to hurt your feelings right now, but that's messed up. You need good friends around you right now to point out what you're not seeing clearly right now, love. Stand up. Push those doubts aside. And trust your decision to leave. Be centered on you because you deserve it.

Let's just get down to brass tacks and give you some advice for the next time you're missing him:

<u>10 THINGS TO DO WHEN YOU MISS YOUR ASSHOLE</u>

1. Phone a friend.
2. Remind yourself he doesn't deserve you (can't touch this).
3. Focus on others (write thank you notes, reconnect with a long-lost friend, do volunteer work, bake cookies for someone "just because")
4. Go for a walk or run in nature.
5. Turn your struggle over to God, source, the universe, or whatever you choose to call your higher power. Meditate & pray.
6. Indulge in self-care (pedicure, hot bath, massage, etc.)
7. Get creative and express your feelings (songwriting, painting, writing poetry, etc.)
8. Do something special for your children or family members.

9. Get in the kitchen and prepare your favorite meal. Better yet, host a dinner party.

10. Enjoy a glass of wine with a friend.

Chapter 16
Inside Their Mind: 5 Things They Hate

Having insight into your opponent's psyche and mindset always puts you in a position of strength. Understanding their weaknesses and tendencies is almost as good as having a peek at their playbook in affording you the ability to predict their behavior.

To that end, and with the purpose of enlightening you about your narcissist's behavior, here are the things assholes hate the most:

1. **Abandonment & rejection**: They can't stand it, to the point it throws them into a rage. To reject a narcissist is the ultimate offense in their view. They continuously feed off the attention of others. When you reject them, they are alone and they hate that. *They* can use and discard *you*, but you're never to do the same to them.

2. **Being made fun of**: Assholes have no sense of humor when the humor is directed at them. They are extremely sensitive and making fun of them is not a laughing matter. To poke fun at a narcissist can be very dangerous. Speak your mind, but have a fast horse, if you know what I mean. They only have a sense of humor at the expense of other people.

3. **Being disrespected**: Assholes are terrified about personal attacks.

It's *your* job to puff them up. They believe they are superior to others and they demand respect.

4. **Being ignored**: This really gets under their skin because they view themselves as all important. They would rather be hated than ignored. In fact, they get off on pushing your buttons, i.e. making you sad, or insecure, or angry. They love to trigger emotions in us. By ignoring them and giving them no supply at all, they die a slow painful death. Their worst fear is being completely irrelevant. When we ghost them, move on, don't miss them, refuse to react and don't care anymore, they are deflated. Responding to their button pushing in a calm manner will throw them off center and annoy them.

5. **Exposure:** Calling them out on their bad behavior or abuse is very dangerous territory. They will become very angry when their behavior is exposed to others.

Chapter 17
11 Step Plan to Healing

The only way to successfully leave an asshole is to truly heal from the experience. The goal is to begin to restore you to make you healthy and whole, so you can then successfully, and without regret, leave your asshole.

I dare say, at the end of your healing you will no longer refer to your asshole with the same venom you did at the beginning of your journey. You will (*gasp*, I know this is hard to believe) begin to look upon your asshole with sympathy and love and a don't-care attitude as to whether he ever comes back and apologizes. You simply won't care, I promise you. And you can still love him.

Our focus now is simple, really. Our plan is to make you stronger in the four important areas of wellness: physically, emotionally, mentally, and spiritually. We need equal balance, focus and strength in these four areas to stand strong.

You could say you really need to work on one area, and throw your effort in to that area (say getting healthy physically, or working on your mindset, or praying more). You could feel like that's the most important area where you need to make changes in your life, to make your life better. But the truth is, you have to achieve balance in all four of those areas.

And the most important area is spiritually. The spiritual path is the path of the heart and the foundation for healing. The spiritual path is the most important area of our focus.

Tuning in spiritually is all about becoming aware of this vibrational universe we live in and how our energy and thoughts affect what we attract in our life. Whether you are aware of it or not, there are spiritual laws that govern life. These spiritual laws are often shunned by the world as woo-woo. However, when they are embraced, you will experience miracles in your life and it will be possible to come out of your broken relationship with your heart more open and loving than ever before. The worst experience of your life will become the source of your greatest spiritual awakening.

These healing steps will help you in the following ways:

- bring positivity and peace into your life…
- help you understand the law of attraction and how thought-by-thought we can attract exactly what we want into our lives…
- teach you how to stop attracting things you don't want in your life…
- teach you what it means to be in alignment and exactly how to get there…
- teach you how to catch yourself and instantly make corrections when you fall out of alignment
- teach you how to forgive, when that's the last thing you want to do…
- help you get control of your life back…
- show you how to enjoy an inspired life full of abundance, joy and freedom…

- and give you a path to being gloriously victorious over the pain and suffering inflicted by your asshole.

When you're living in alignment, you're inspired. You feel clarity and patience and happiness and fullness and passion and flow. You also feel love and appreciation. These are all the feelings you experience when you're in alignment. If you're not feeling all those feelings, you know you're out of alignment. If you're longing for something, if you feel stuck, depressed - what you're really looking for is alignment. These steps will help you find inspiration and move back into alignment.

These steps are the very things I started doing daily, in earnest, when I set off on my journey to healing. Once I started doing these things I began to sleep better and immediately had greater peace. I can tell you I have more energy today because of these things. I feel better, I'm physically healthier, I'm more fit, I breathe more deeply, I feel mentally stronger than I have in a long time and I also feel love and forgiveness towards the people in my life who cause me stress, including my asshole and his flying monkeys. I have a profound sense of peace that I didn't have before and I hope you find the same.

Ready to get started?

Chapter 18
Step 1: We Are What We Think – Choose Carefully

"Your thoughts create your life."

Wayne Dyer

The brilliant philosopher and motivational speaker Wayne Dyer spent his lifetime teaching people that thought-by-thought we create our life and what happens in our life. Admittedly, it took me a while to fully understand this.

Dyer explained the ancestor to every action in our life is a thought. The ancestor to everything in life, as a matter of fact – everything that is ever done or created - is first a mere thought. Every invention was first a thought in someone's mind before it became a reality. The light bulb was first a thought conceived in the mind of Thomas Edison before it actually existed. The airplane was first an idea that was conceived and then designed before it was built. The wheel was a thought in the minds of cavemen before it was created (did cavemen invent the wheel??... I need to google that). Anyway, everything that has ever been invented or created in this life was first just imagined. Everything was first a thought.

Everything you've done today – made coffee, ran errands, drove to work - was first a thought in your mind. Everything you've ever done and accomplished in your life that you're proud of was first just a thought in your mind. Everything you've done that you're not proud of was first a thought

Before we do anything, we first think about it. There's never an action taken without a thought preceding it. Thoughts come first. And so, your life always follows the direction of your thinking.

So, what kind of thoughts are you filling your mind with?

Do you have negative thoughts, and are you full of fear and anger?

Are you thinking about how you can change the world in a positive way?

Are you dwelling on what you lack in your life right now?

Are you thinking about how you have a bright, loving future and you will be victorious in your healing from your current situation?

Are you thinking, "this is a scary hurtful world"…?

There's a natural law in the universe, called the "law of attraction" that says our thoughts determine the quality and content of our life. That is, what you focus on expands.

The law of attraction says you attract and manifest in your life what you think about and focus on:

Happy thoughts attract happy things.

Hateful thoughts attract more hate.

Gratefulness attracts more things to be grateful for.

Loving thoughts attract more things to be joyful for

Worry attracts more worry.

Fear attracts more fear.

Anger attracts more anger.

If you think this is a loving world and people are good, then that's what the universe delivers.

If you think you're surrounded by dishonest people who are out to get you and you think the world is full of uncertainty and things to be afraid of, again, that's what the universe delivers.

The law of attraction is always in effect, much like the law of gravity. Whether you believe it exists or not, that doesn't change the fact it's real and affects our lives.

Thought by thought we create our life and choose to be in alignment. Our energy and our vibration comes from our thoughts and focus. What manifests in our life all goes back to single individual thoughts.

If you want love, have loving thoughts.

If you want peace, have peaceful thoughts.

The universe answers your thoughts and vibrations with exactly what you're feeling and thinking about. Even the Bible says, "as you think, so shall you be."

If you constantly think about what you lack - that's what you will attract. If you constantly dwell on being victimized, you will attract more of that into your life. If you are inspired and hopeful, you will attract positive things. It's important to understand the law of attraction.

You must focus on positive and healthy thoughts to attract positive and healthy things into your life. If you focus on sadness and negativity then that's what you attract in your life.

Reject feelings of fear, if you don't want fear.

Reject feelings of anger, if you don't want more anger in your life.

It's no secret our bodies respond to our thoughts. Think of the toll stressful thoughts have on your body… racing heart, headaches, and more. Lie detector tests work on the premise of measuring your body's response to thoughts. Even Pavlov's dogs proved a link between a dog thinking of food and their bodies responding. There is a proven link that biologically; we think and our bodies respond. Our bodies are influenced by our thoughts.

Similarly, the universe responds to our thoughts. What you think is your request to the universe to send more of the same, and the universe responds. It sends you more of the same vibration you're sending out. Have you ever thought of someone and then you see them? Our thoughts have the ability to prompt someone to reach out to us. The stronger the thoughts, the stronger the pull.

Thoughts are energy. They are not fluffy little inconsequential things. They have power. They are real. Those positive and negative thoughts you have and actions you take based on them determine the direction of your life takes, so choose positive ones.

It's also important to release negative thoughts to attract what you want. Not only do negative thoughts attract more negative energy but they also block positive energy. When you ruminate on the bad things your asshole has done, you're staying stuck in that place where you attract negative energy and block the positive. I'm not saying don't feel the pain of what has happened, it's just important to *not unpack and stay in that place.*

When you encounter something negative, curb the impulse to react negatively to it. If you react negatively (say, get angry), that's requesting more of the same. Instead, think differently and focus on what you want.

It's like tuning a radio. You may over shoot. Try again. Dial it back. Your frequency has to be the same as what you want to attract. It's a skill to learn. If you want love and peace, you need to be in harmony with those things. You can't be angry. That's a different frequency. Make sure you're sending out the energy that is the same frequency of what you want.

If you have angry energy, you will attract more angry energy.

If you are fearful and skeptical, you will attract those negative energies.

Choose what you want, sweet girl.

Just remember, what is best for you is being in alignment. It's also best for anyone who is around you.

How do I know if I'm in alignment?

Oh, you will know! It will be an unmistakable feeling. You will feel joyful and excited. You will feel connected and energetic and optimistic. You will feel you are doing what you are meant to do. That's the universe telling you you're in alignment! When we're in alignment with God everything unfolds with ease and a pureness. We are happy, excited, and passionate.

When you are being guided by the universe, there's a sense of peace. When it's your own hands doing the guiding, it feels heavy and burdensome. It's a light and positive feeling when the universe is guiding you. You can feel the difference.

Once you experience alignment and learn to recognize it, we always want to be back there. There's nothing like the feeling when you are vibrating at a high frequency. You're doing something that brings you joy, makes you happy and gives you a sense of purpose. All those feelings raise your vibrational energy. When we are in alignment, the universe also supports us completely and opens doors for us, bringing miracles and blessings. It's hard not to notice the miracles and blessings!

How do I know if I'm not in alignment?

Again, you know it. You have a feeling that something is wrong. You're also not at peace. Everything falls apart.

When was the last time you were happy? Excited? In love with life? What were you doing? Who were you with? Were you at peace? Were you excited about what you were doing? The reason you were excited was because you were aligned with your purpose. That's the path you were supposed to be on. Everything that excited you and made you feel good was alignment. That's flow. Positive feelings are an indication that we are staying aligned and are on the right path. Negative feelings are an indication that we're not aligned and are not on the right path.

How do we get back to alignment if we've lost it?

We all experience "wobbles" (a term coined by spiritual speaker and author Esther Hicks to refer to the times when we fall out of alignment). To get back in alignment, you need to match your frequency to what you want to dial in. You have to raise your frequency in order to tune in alignment. To raise your frequency, it's all in your thoughts. Change your thoughts.

Giving your attention to something negative for a brief amount of time, is not a troublesome thing. When you give your attention to something negative regularly and daily and for long periods of time, then a vibrational reality is formed around that. The law of attraction is listening and responding to those thoughts. Be very careful.

So, how do we raise our vibrational energy?

It's all in our thoughts. Our thoughts lead to our feelings, and our feelings affect our vibrational frequency. It all starts with thoughts. You must keep your thoughts in the positive range. Choose hope, choose happiness, choose optimism, choose joy, love, acceptance, and appreciation. Feel those emotions. We have to be very deliberate in (1) choosing and focusing on more positive thoughts and, (2) releasing negative thoughts.

How do I change my thoughts?

- positive self-talk
- affirmations
- meditation
- having a heart of gratitude
- visualization
- tuning into the spiritual world

Have you ever met someone whom you had an instant feeling there was something wrong with them? Your discernment screamed this person was not to be trusted and something was off? It's as if they were emitting a vibration that was unhealthy and bad. And they were!

You picked up on something very real. Your vibration clashed with the vibration of that person and not only were you not attracted to them, but you were repelled. Your vibrational energies didn't match and you felt and heard that loud and clear!

Alternatively, I know you have experienced being in love. That excited exhilarated feeling when you were full of clarity and hope and your mind expanded in all directions with love and trust. You were in this wonderful world, in touch with your purpose and your true self. Endless possibilities were visible. You were in flow and in alignment and you moved in the direction of love and all things positive. Have you also noticed that when you do what you love, energy and abundance seems to flow and when you're in love, you fall more deeply in love?

When you were in love, there was profound peace that you were in sync, and it felt wonderful to you and to your partner, too. It was as if you were magnetically attracted, and you were! Energetically you both were emitting the same vibrations that firmly planted you in that place where we originated from – God and source energy. Whenever we return to the one who created us (call it what you prefer: God, the divine, source, the universe) the more we are in alignment. That's when flow sets in. Once you have a taste of that, you will always long for it. God's energy is driving the relationship. Everything opens up when two people who are spiritually connected come together and turn in the direction of love. It's a powerful thing!

So, what exactly went wrong with my asshole? I experienced that flow and feeling of love with my asshole and was wildly attracted, and then everything went horribly wrong? What about that?

I wondered the same thing myself.

What happens is, the flow gets buried and disappears when one person strays from source, that God-centered place where we are in alignment and at peace. Sometimes people never learn how to restore themselves and merely drift further and further away.

The asshole becomes a misguided person who drifts away from all that is good to the chaos of the world that's selfish, greedy and blaming. They move to the "I know what's best" world where selfishness rules, things matter more than people, they don't trust anyone, and what's most important in life is what they want. They care only about their own selfish desires.

When we deviate from love and stubbornly position ourselves at a vantage point of selfishness and distrust, we are far from the essence of who we are.

Unfortunately, you can't love someone back into alignment, back from evil to love. They have to do it themselves. You must be hands-off and you can't do it for them (I know that's hard for an empath). It's not your job to get them back there. Spiritual journeys must be taken alone. The only way for them to realign is to return to alignment on their own. You need to save yourself first.

Question: *So, I'm working on being in alignment and my thoughts, but it's not working. I love him and I miss him terribly. He's gone and I need him in my life. I will do anything to get him back. What can I do?*

A: Here's what I hear you saying (i.e. what your thoughts are):

I miss him.
I miss him terribly.
He's gone and I want him to come back.
He's left a big hole in my life.

Your entire vibration is different from what you want. You have to feel like you feel when you have what you want. How did it feel when you were first with asshole and in love? Remember back to the first time you made love. Back to the core of when you were in sync and things were wonderful. What did that feel like? When you were in-sync, trusting, loving, hopeful and close to source. Don't focus on what's missing! Focus on what you want.

And then assume the feeling of having what you want, feel the feeling of having what your heart desires. A vibrational reality is formed from your thoughts, so make them positive. You have to do the vibrational work. You have to build the momentum to what you want in your life. If you feel it, the universe will open doors for you. Just don't be surprised if what the universe brings you is not him. You want happiness and joy, and the universe will bring that to you, but maybe in the form of someone else. It will bring you something better that will give you that feeling.

That's how to be in vibrational alignment with what you want. That's what you need to do for the universe to deliver what you want. That's the work. That's the secret. The law of attraction will help you. Trust it.

Simply align with what you're asking for and assume the feeling of it; it will come! Choose your thoughts carefully. Once you do that, the universe is on it. You can sit back and know that what you desire is manifesting behind the scenes. So, the power to create your life is in your hands. It's about tuning into alignment.

And, don't be trying to make things happen yourself "behind the scenes." Once you get in alignment and flow opens up, the universe will deliver what you desire right to you. Let it all come to you. And keep reminding yourself it's coming.

Chapter 19
Step 2: Establish Morning & Evening Routines

One of the best things I've ever done to re-center and reset my life was to develop a morning routine. I'm a firm believer sometimes you need a clean slate and a fresh start… hitting the reset button, so to speak. And nothing helps you reset your life better and more quickly than a morning routine that makes you wake up with energy and a sense of purpose and positivity.

The book that originally turned me on to the importance of morning routines was, *The Miracle Morning: The Not-So-Obvious Secret Guaranteed to Transform Your Life Before 8am,* by Hal Elrod. It's a book that will inspire you to make changes in your life and use your mornings to turn your life around and kick-start your goals. Of all the books I've read in the last few years, it's one of the books I buy most to give as a gifts to people who are looking for a super-fast reset in their lives.

According to the book, Hal Elrod says changing your mornings can change your whole life and he outlines how your morning should consist of six simple activities:

1. Silence

2. Affirmations

3. Visualization
4. Exercise
5. Reading
6. Scribing (journaling, in other words)

I have applied many of these principles in my morning routine.

One area where I deviated from Hal's advice though, has to do with the alarm clock I use to wake up. I'm not a big fan of traditional alarm clocks or using my phone as an alarm. And, his suggestion to put your alarm on the other side of the room where you sleep (forcing you clear out of bed to turn it off) is a huge turn off for me. Today I don't even use an alarm clock. Ever. I've totally changed my falling-asleep and waking-up habits where I don't use jarring alarms and, instead, I wake up slowly and naturally.

Instead of an alarm clock, I have equipped my bedroom with a Philips Hue smart LED lighting system. You can actually use the bulbs and system throughout your house if you like, but I started in the bedroom and that's where it's made a huge difference for me. One little bridge controls up to 50 light bulbs. And it lets you turn off-and-on the lights at various times and program them to turn off when you go to bed or when you leave the room and even change the color of your lighting. They're also controlled by an app that's compatible with Apple Home Kit, Amazon Alexa, Google Home and more. But that's not why I love the Hue light bulbs. Let me explain.

I wake up gently feeling like I slept in. And, I wake up to a fully lit room. Whatever time I want to wake up, I program the lights to what time I want to be awake, and then 20 to 30 minutes before that time, the light or lights gradually come on. By the time they're all the way on, my brain has very gently been pulled out of sleep and I'm awake and feeling refreshed. I don't think I'll ever go back to a traditional alarm clock, ever.

Also, at bedtime, you can adjust the light to a tone that makes you very relaxed and sleepy (I love-love-love that!). And, all the lights can be controlled by my voice. I can get in bed and with one simple voice command, turn off the hall light or all the lights in my bedroom. And then wake up at a slow pace, gradually coming out of REM sleep and feeling wonderful. It's a more natural soothing way of waking up.

And I make the rest of my morning routine equally nurturing and uplifting. I don't wake up and immediately check Facebook, email and voicemails on my phone. Instead, I spend time relaxing and reflecting on what's good in my life. Every day I get up, I drink a bottle of water and then eat a healthy breakfast and drink coffee. I then workout (go to the gym or do yoga). I take vitamins, I meditate and I read affirmations.

Here's the morning routine I use to set the tone for my day:

1. Drink a glass of water.

I do this before I even get up out of bed. The night before, I set a 16 fl. oz. bottle of water on my nightstand. And I drink it as soon as I wake up. Or, fill an aluminum thermos with ice and water the night before and drink that. I've been doing this for a couple years now and it makes a huge difference in how I feel. I don't know if it's hydrating your body first thing in the morning that is such a brilliant pick-me-up, or if it's the coolness of the water. No matter, I believe this is a healthy habit to stick with.

2. Meditate.

Meditation is what Hal Elrod in *The Miracle Morning* refers to as purposeful silence and he points out that this can be a powerful stress-reliever in our lives. He says doing it for as little as 60 seconds is of huge benefit (I would bump that up to 5 minutes myself). I meditate for a minimum of 20 minutes twice a day (and often more). I can't tell you enough, I've noticed a *huge* difference in my life (in the amount of peace and clarity and calmness I enjoy when I do meditate as opposed to when

I don't). It really does make a huge difference in how you feel and clarity of mind.

3. Eat a healthy breakfast.

I eat some protein, usually some eggs or bacon. And coffee. Lots of coffee. I'm a huge fan of Bulletproof coffee... something you've probably heard of if you're in to biohacking or in the keto or paleo crowd. I don't always add the butter and brain octane oil, but I swear by how great I feel when I do. I feel amazing, full of energy and ready to take on the world.

4. Work-out.

Five-days-a-week I something to exercise. I either go to the gym to workout, take my dog for a walk or run, or do yoga. I love going to the gym to work out, working out, coming home and getting a shower, and starting my day feeling energized. Whatever your thing is you love to do for exercising, whether it's a short walk or run on a treadmill, just find your thing and commit to doing it daily.

5. Read affirmations.

Positive affirmations and visualization are a part of my every morning. I wake up and read them on a piece of paper that I have taped to my bathroom mirror. I also have them on my cell phone. When I'm on the treadmill, I flip through them and feed my spirit with positive statements.

By the way, affirmations can come in other forms. I also read affirming and positive books, read affirming social media posts, and surround myself with affirming people.

I also make sure that my own self talk is affirming. Instead of ruminating, "*My asshole has ruined my life*" or "*I'm never going to be happy again, I'm never going to find love again*" I think affirming thoughts.

Try writing down some of the following positive affirmations:

I am focused on becoming healthy and balanced.

My positive and loving outlook attracts positive people around me.

I am committed to working out 5-days-a-week.

I am going to successfully complete my 100-day clean eating challenge.

Create your own positive affirmations and read them every morning. You are not only programming your mind to achieve those goals, you're visualizing your success.

There is a study I once heard about where a group of people were gathered and told to visualize throwing darts at a bulls-eye target. The people never touched an actual dart and they never practiced for real. All they did was visualize themselves throwing darts at a target and, as they were instructed to do, they visualized themselves hitting the bulls-eye target dead-on in the center.

When darts were finally given to these people who had been mentally practicing, they were really fantastic at hitting the target. They were almost as good as the people who actually practiced throwing real darts at actual targets. The mental practicing was almost as good as real life practicing. Visualization is powerful.

So, as you create and write out your own daily affirmations, be sure to include things that you will visualize yourself doing successfully. Tell yourself you will do these things. Tell yourself you will be successful doing those things and then get on to reading them daily and believing they are manifesting.

Keep it positive! Make this part of your daily thoughts! Write them on post-it notes, spread them around the house, on the refrigerator, on your computer monitor, everywhere. Make your background image on your phone be the cover of the book you're going to write (I did that with this book and now it's a reality)! The idea is to constantly see these positive messages and burn them into your psyche.

Need help creating your own affirmations? Consider these:

Life is full of love and I find it everywhere I go.

I am confident and happy.

I am excited and feel fully and freely alive.

I greet each second of life with enthusiasm and hope.

I wake up happy and excited every day.

I choose to see the goodness in other people.

I am present in every moment.

I do not have to prove myself to anyone.

6. Express gratitude.

Every morning, before I sit down to work, I write down three things I'm thankful for in my life. It can be anything… something that happened yesterday, a person in my life I love, a good meal, a warm bed, anything. Studies show that there are many benefits realized when you live in a spirit of gratitude.

And so that's my morning!

There are some other morning routines I have experimented with, including cold showers. At one time, I studied Wim Hof and his findings about the health benefits of cold showers. We're talking serious health benefits and how we should all take a 15 to 30 second ice cold showers every day. Or, submerge your face in a pan of ice cold water (I know, this sounds insane). As crazy and goofy as it sounds, I did try this, and I did feel energized and awake (no, duh) after a cold shower, but cold showers are definitely not my cup of tea. But if you're into extreme bio-hacking and maximizing performance, perhaps it's something you should look into.

Tailor your morning routine to suit you. In the same way that I read and researched many ideas and suggestions for a morning routine, you should do the same. Choose a morning routine that works for you and makes you wake up energized with purpose and positivity.

And feel free to vary your morning routine. Sometimes, I like to switch things up and exercise in the afternoon. Sometimes, I like to work-out twice in one day. Sometimes, I meditate for 20 minutes in the morning and sometimes I meditate for only 10 minutes.

I don't like to be so rigid with the routine. I like to be more open and flexible and have the freedom to change things, but I'm very consistent and intentional in what I do and how I spend my time these days. Some mornings, I immediately put on my workout clothes and head out the door to the gym. Other mornings, I make breakfast and then meditate.

Jump in, take action today and get started! Start working on your own personal morning routine. Before you go to bed tonight, get excited about tomorrow, make a layout of a preliminary morning routine and what you want to get done, decide how you want to meditate tomorrow (using an app? a YouTube video?), how you are going to exercise, and have your list of affirmations ready to go.

Evening is a great time to get ready for tomorrow. I'll even argue that your evening routine is perhaps, the most important routine of the day. You need one of those too… an evening routine.

Those last minutes of your day are so important as you're getting ready to go to sleep. Wayne Dyer, the famous self-help author and spiritual coach, taught a lot on this subject during his lifetime and he explained that as you're getting ready to go to sleep, whatever you're thinking about, whatever your thoughts are before you go to sleep, that's what you're going to "marinate in" for the next eight hours.

So, what are you thinking about when you go to bed? Are you fretting about what you didn't get done today? Are you ruminating on something horrible your asshole did today? Are you worrying about what you need to get done tomorrow? Are you re-living something bad?

If those are the thoughts you're "marinating in" as you go to sleep and your subconscious mind takes over, you're not in a good place. The subconscious mind is very susceptible and busy at work while you're sleeping, and it's feeding on that information.

Dyer taught that in that last five minutes before you go to bed, don't program your mind, fill your mind with all the things you don't' want in your life, or the things that aren't working out. Instead, fill your mind with positive thoughts!

Fill your mind with positive affirmations… things like *I am strong, I am happy, I'm healthy, I am kind.* Not *I am sick, I'm unhappy, I'm lonely, I'm tired, I'm struggling.* You don't want to manifest those things in your life, so change your thinking. Manifest the things you *do* want in your life by thinking and focusing on those things. Fall asleep thinking about and assuming the feeling of the things that you DO want. That's how to attract those things.

Think about how it would feel if your wish was realized. That's what you want to think about as you're slipping off to sleep. *I am healthy, I am content, I am happy.* You have to feel the wish fulfilled to call it to you.

So, my bedtime routine is simply this, it's meditating and doing some positive affirmations. I also take magnesium sometimes to help my body relax at bedtime. I interviewed Tony Robbins several years ago for an article I wrote about becoming a morning person and I learned so much from Tony that day. He taught me about the importance of magnesium in your diet and how it's a very natural way to relax your body to help you fall asleep.

So, figure out what works for you in the evenings, set a routine, follow through with the routine and go to sleep. Having programmed your mind properly, you will marinate your subconscious in positive thoughts. Sweet dreams!

Chapter 20
Step 3: Protect Your Time & Energy Like a Mama Bear

Many precede and many will follow
A young girl's dreams no longer hollow
It takes the shape of a place out west
But what it holds for her, she hasn't yet guessed
She needs wide open spaces.

Susan Gibson

From now on, you need to become fiercely protective of the resources in your life: your time, your energy, and your space. Become intentional about protecting all three in equal measure so that they serve your healing plan. Stop giving endlessly with no regard to your own dreams and goals, and your body's need for rest. Boundaries are healthy. Excess in any area of our life is most definitely *not* healthy.

Here are some ways to protect your time and surroundings so that you have the margin in your life to focus on you. Here goes…

Say "no" at least once a day!

People pleasers to the core, we empaths have a hard time saying "no." If asked to do something we don't want to do, we'll say "yes." If invited to attend an event we really don't want to attend, we'll cave and answer, "sure." Learning to say "no" is very hard for us.

In the future, when you feel pulled to say "yes" when you want to say "no" - do it! It's a lovely thing to say no. It's okay to choose to stay home. It's okay to not accept every invitation. It's okay to want to be alone. It's also okay to let a phone call go to voice mail. And, it's okay to not provide any explanation or apology.

You're not being rude or missing out—you're making a choice. It's called putting yourself first and focusing on getting healthy.

Start setting clear boundaries and put your needs first. Break those bad habits of endlessly being available. Take control of your precious time. We all need to become gleefully comfortable saying "no" (*"no, no, no, no, no!")* ... let your voice ring out like a little defiant toddler!

How liberating it is get your time back! We need to start spending our time in a way that best serves *us*, with a focus on *our* goals and time spent with *our* cherished family members and friends.

Go on a retreat.

> This can be done in a number of ways: a day spent at the library, an afternoon at a corner table in a coffee shop, getting away for a weekend either by yourself or with someone else, or get away for a longer period of time. I went away for two months and made it a time of thinking, reflecting, planning, and healing.
>
> I worked on goals, I did a lot of reading, I listened to lectures, I devoured self-improvement materials, I attended workshops, I met with people, and I visited art museums in various cities (for relaxation and inspiration). I also did a deep-dive study into

researching the world's great spiritual leaders through different cultural lenses. I studied Buddhism, Taoism, and my own Christianity (despite having encountered one or two wretched counterfeit Christians during my most difficult time).

Going on a retreat affords you the time and space to focus on YOU and is a great way to hit the reset button. It offers you a chance to get out of your ordinary environment and break the routine and be deliberate about how you spend your time and reset.

Declutter your home. Quite literally create space for yourself to breathe and focus. Minimize. Minimize. Minimize. Less stuff means less stress. Get rid of things you don't need. You'll be amazed at the affect clearing out "stuff" has on your psyche.

If you don't know where to start, take a cue from Marla Cilley, aka The FlyLady. Tackle it in 15 minute increments. She says we can do anything for 15 minutes. And, you will feel so much better making your space, your home, your nightstand, and your bedroom perfect for you.

Be organized with where you place your belongings. We add to our stress when we can't find things. And our minds function best when we are free of mind clutter and free from worry and stress.

Spend 15 minutes a day on a project you're passionate about.

Maybe that project you've been wanting to start is writing a book. Maybe you want to research starting a business, or get involved with a local charity. It could be anything. No matter what the project, start devoting 15 minutes a day to the effort. Get started and you will be surprised at the momentum that builds. Spending 15 minutes a day tackling projects can bring unbelievable transformation to your life (again, thank you FlyLady!). No longer will old habits short circuit your success.

Map out new goals!

What goals have you been putting off for too long? Losing weight? Getting healthy?

What are your passions?

What do you want your legacy to be?

What do you want to accomplish?

Enjoy the process of thinking and considering the types of things you wish to pursue and achieve for yourself, and then narrow down the list to three of four concrete goals.

Tip: Mind-mapping is a fun way to help brainstorm ideas. Get a pad of post-it notes and start scribbling down a free flow of ideas of things you dream about and see yourself passionately pursuing and achieving. Mind-mapping is a genius and fast way to sort through your thoughts!

Finally, narrow down your goals in list form. Do you know that you are 42% more likely to achieve your goals just by writing them down? A study by Dr. Gail Matthews of Dominican University found this extra step kick-starts our brains into building resolve and accomplishing our goals.

After you create your list of goals, develop a plan for achieving them. This involves (1) looking at what resources you have available to help you achieve your goal and (2) then creating a plan. The more we intentionally focus and take steps toward our goals the more we will be motivated to achieve them.

Let's say your goal is as follows:

Goal: I want to lose fifteen pounds.

What are all the resources available to you?

- Access to a gym
- Neighborhood where you can run/walk
- Pool
- Exercise shoes & workout clothes
- Weight scale
- Your doctor for advice and guidance
- Help from a nutritionist for meal planning?
- A fitness trainer?

Given these resources, make a concrete plan:

- I'm going to make the following changes to my diet (no fried foods, no sugar, no bread, counting calories, fasting for 16 hours each day, etc.). You decide your plan.
- I'm going to commit to exercising (5 days a week, 15 minutes a day, twice a week, 40 minutes of cardio followed by weight training, running 3 miles a day, whatever you decide).

  When you set your sights on a goal, get excited and take on the energy of it. Get moving on it!
- Be visual with your goals! Visually write goals out in a place where you will continually see them throughout your day (on the wall using large poster sized post-it sheets, on pieces of paper taped to your mirror, on your computer desktop, phone background, etc.).

Also, get a large calendar and track your progress. Place it in a highly visible place and make at least one action every day toward your goal.

Implement a daily to-do list.

Plan ahead exactly what tasks need to be done each day and how you will spend your time. Prioritize tasks. And, at the end of every day, plan for tomorrow. If you're at work, map out your next day's tasks before you go home. What tasks need to be done each day to make progress on your goals?

One of my challenges is finding time to get everything done. I've used everything from calendar apps to paper calendars to track my daily things-to-do. Doing so helps me plan my day and make progress. Having a system reduces stress and makes everything easier.

Chapter 21
Step 4: Let Go of the Need for a Specific Outcome

We empaths are fixers. We know how to set things right. We know what we want to see happen and how to get there. We're planners and we're confident in in our ability to see a problem and help with a fix, and we double our efforts to get the outcome we want. We've lived our whole world in that space.

We base our happiness on pleasing our asshole, dancing and navigating and obsessing in order to keep him happy and steady the ship. Face it girl, we're "A+ students" in allowing the outward conditions of our life to dictate everything in our world. So, this step won't come easy.

The problem with always basing our happiness on a specific outcome that we think is under our control, is that it only leads to unhappiness. Happiness doesn't come from our assholes. It comes from within our heart.

> "We must learn to let go. Release the stress.
> You were never in control anyway."
>
> *Steve Maraboli*

Instead of always affecting the outcome of everything, take your hands off the wheel and allow things to unfold the way they're supposed to unfold. We're going to be okay no matter what happens. Trust everything is happening for your highest good. Release your timeframe. Over-obsessing on a specific outcome will only lead to misery. Be the opposite of your controlling asshole.

Have a mindset that is open to anything and attached to nothing at the same time. And, I get it. It's easy to be unattached to any outcome when you're happy. It's harder to do when you're unhappy.

You're feeling overwhelmed and hopeless. Our plans with prince charming didn't play out as hoped. We're hurting. And, things only seem to be getting worse. But, the more we accept everything as it is and are less rigid, the happier we will be. We have to trust that the divine is ON IT for us. Things are, indeed, manifesting for us. It's only when we stop pushing so hard and trying to control things that wonderful things happen. Our job is to let go of the need for a specific outcome in our life. Then, the universe will then deliver more than we ever imagined. Instead of focusing on controlling the outcome, release control and focus on being in alignment and flow.

The symphonies that the brilliant composer Mozart created just came to him. He didn't stress and obsess about the next note he was to write on the staff on his paper. It all flowed to him effortlessly when he allowed himself to receive whatever flowed to him naturally.

Answers and blessings will come to us as long as we're willing to listen and let them come, instead of our hands creating them. You let the great spirit take over and you release to it. You submit to it. We get in the way of ourselves when we try to affect the outcome. Be present in the moment and listen and release instead.

Shift into surrender energy. Embrace complete acceptance of what is. In surrender, you will experience peace and an in-the-moment calm. Just as in facing uncomfortable thoughts and emotions face-on and burning them up, by facing our attachments and fully accepting that they don't serve us, we can give them up. Therein, lies freedom, sweet girl!

Worksheet #8

What specific outcomes are you attached to and obsessing about?

Worksheet #9

What are some of the things you're worrying about?

Worksheet #10

What other attachments do you have?

Chapter 22
Step 5: Take Care of Your Body

Quite simply, make health and fitness a priority in your life. Take responsibility for your physical wellbeing. This involves (1) staying active, (2) minding what we eat and drink, and (3) making sure you see a doctor through this life-changing devastating time you're going through.

1. Stay active!

And, no excuses for not being able to think of how to exercise. Here are 40 fun ways to get moving and get some exercise:

- Dance to music on your phone
- Take a yoga class
- Clean your house
- Take the stairs instead of the elevator
- Do jumping jacks
- Jump rope
- Go for a hike
- Work in the garden

- Take a walk
- Google "body weight" exercises (and do them!)
- Go walk your local shopping mall
- Mow your yard
- Go bowling
- Play a workout video game
- Exercise with your dog
- Play Frisbee
- Take a spin class
- Play basketball
- Go paddle boarding
- Try Pilates
- Download a fitness app & workout
- Planking
- Go for a run
- Indoor rock climbing
- Take a walking tour of your city
- Hoola hoop
- Go to the gym for a workout
- Do cartwheels
- Go geocaching

- Horseback riding
- Play on a playground
- Go to the driving range
- Take some swings at a batting cage
- Do a workout video
- Go zip-lining
- Ride a bike
- Go swimming
- Go Kayaking, canoeing or rafting
- Kickboxing
- Take a Zumba class

Karen Jones, fitness instructor and author of *"Happy You Happy Body"* is an inspiring woman I follow daily for fitness motivation and advice. She's been very open about her own struggle in overcoming a toxic relationship and she continues to influence me daily on social media. Find quality influencers in the fitness space and follow them.

2. Mind what we eat and drink:

We are what we eat and drink, so let's get serious about what we're putting into our bodies. A healthy diet is foundational to our healing.

Let's break this down. I'm going to propose another way of looking at improving our diet without turning it into a regimented diet. Of course, that's an option. We can start a diet and be extremely regimented and I've done that. Last year, my version of a regimented diet was a self-imposed 100-day "clean eating challenge" that consisted of:

- no processed foods (that was easy for me)

- no sugar (that was a little bit harder)
- no fried foods
- no bread

I will be honest and tell you I am not good at rigidly adhering to a diet. I just want what I want when I want it. Sometimes, I just wanted bread. Sometimes, I just wanted a hamburger. Sometimes, I wanted dessert. I would say I followed the 80/20 rule. 80% of the time, I was on the program and I enjoyed it and 20% of the time I just wanted to color outside of the lines because I don't like having to adhere to a strict diet. I like balance. I don't like rigidity.

This year instead of doing any 100-day clean eating challenges, I have determined to focus wholly on adding as many quality, nutrient rich foods to my diet as possible; tons of veggies, greens, good fats, and organics. And I figure if I do that, it will crowd out the bad stuff that I want to eat. After all, when I eat the good stuff, I feel so much better and I have so much energy. I don't want any of the bad stuff, so no diets for me this year.

I'm focusing on quality foods but more importantly, I'm focusing on the power of alkalinity on my health. And once you learn about alkalinity, that will change the way you eat and give you amazing energy.

So, there's this thing in your body called alkaline acidic balance. Just like your body maintains your body's temperature, and there's an ideal temperature for maintaining sound health, there's another important number in your body and that's pH. It's is measured on a scale from 0 to 14 and it measures how acidic or how alkaline your body is. So, 7 is neutral, 14 is extremely alkaline. Your body has to be slightly alkaline at 7.36.

What you need to know is if your body is measuring acidic, you can't lose weight and your body is breaking down. Your body is not getting as much oxygen as it should be. You can be exercising like crazy and think you're doing great, but you're not. If you're measuring acidic you will not lose weight because being acidic slows down your metabolism and the acid gets stored in your fat. Your body's way of protecting itself is to hold on to fat to protect itself against the acid in your body.

If you're measuring your pH and your measuring alkaline, that's a good thing, as microorganisms cannot grow in an alkaline environment. Cancer cannot grow in an alkaline environment.

So, I believe the way you get healthy and clean out your body is to become more alkaline. If you want to lose weight, you want to focus on becoming more alkaline and becoming less acidic. Stop focusing on, "I need to lose weight" and focus instead on "I am too acidic." You need to become more alkaline and watch the difference in your health. Once you get the acid out of your body, your body will let go of the fat it's holding to protect you and you will lose weight.

You can measure your pH, your alkalinity on a regular basis. I use measuring strips you can buy at the health food store. You can test with your urine or you can also do blood test, but of course that's much more involved and complicated.

There are certain foods that you want to eat more of to become more alkaline. Things like greens, almonds, carrots, spinach, avocados, cucumbers, brussels sprouts, and broccoli. And, of course, avoid acidic foods. By far, the worst offender of them all is sugar, so stay away from it as much as possible.

Another important thing to do related to what we eat and drink is detoxing. It's important to learn which foods help detox our body and carry and wash toxins out of our bodies so they aren't reabsorbed. We need to eat more of these detox foods and eat them regularly, foods like cilantro and broccoli and chia seeds.

Chia seeds are amazing. You can add them in smoothies and drinks and you can sneak them in wherever you can. They are gelatinous and as they make their way through your body, they collect toxins and carry them away. Google recipes for chia seeds and next time you're in Whole Foods or Earth Fare, be sure to pick up a small bag of organic chia seeds and start adding a small teaspoon here or there into your diet. They will make a huge difference.

3. Make sure you see a doctor through this difficult time you're going through:

This will undoubtedly be one of the most traumatic experiences you will go through in your life. These are excruciatingly painful experiences. You will experience despair and sadness, depression and thoughts of suicide are also common place. Mentally, you're stretched to your limits. The toll these experiences take on your well-being and body is significant. A doctor can be extremely helpful in making sure you come through the experience intact and healthy.

If you are experiencing abuse or depression, tell your doctor. Explain the personal struggle you're experiencing. Your doctor will be able to help you and needs to know what you're feeling. Sometimes medication is needed to get you through rough patches.

Also, it's important to know that when you're abused and going through what you're going through, it's completely normal to experience despair and sadness and anxiety. Only a sociopath has no feelings, for goodness sake. There's nothing wrong with you. You're upset. What you're feeling is completely normal given your circumstances. Give your mind and heart a chance to heal itself. Don't be ashamed. Share with your doctor.

Chapter 23
Step 6: Tune into Mindfulness

To save the world we must have a plan.
But no plan will work unless we meditate.

Dalai Lama

We live in such a crazy hurried world where many people scoff at the idea of spirituality. That's not the real world, they say. They're focused solely on the physical tangible world, that which you can see and touch and affect. Anything else isn't real.

And yet, spirituality *is* the foundation of our existence. Whether you choose to believe it or not, everything that happens in this world manifests from the spiritual world. It is central to our daily existence. When you recognize only the physical realm of our world, that's where we get stuck.

So, how do we tap into and shore up our spiritual foundation?

The only way to tap into spirituality and the unseen world of vibrational energy is to cultivate mindfulness… and that simply means: meditate. Only when we calm the noise that is around us through silence can we hear the universe (or God, or the divine, or source - whatever you're most comfortable calling it).

The best benefit of quiet meditation is hearing what many call that loving loyal voice that speaks within us all: our inner guidance. You can also call it God's voice, your intuition, our heart. No matter what we call it, it's that voice that if stop and listen, it will guide us. I believe that's why we get so lost when we don't meditate and why things seem to fall into place when we are aligned and when we do practice meditation.

The universe only communicates with quiet peaceful minds. It can never be heard in chaos and where there is conflict. When we learn to stop, reflect, listen and develop a Buddhist mindset we open ourselves to all the rich gifts and miracles that are possible.

I call it meditation. You may call it prayer or simply sitting in silence. Bottom line: Silence is the key. Going into that spiritual realm gives us the mind of God, a mind of love. Through meditation we purify our mind and consciousness and align ourselves with the universe that loves us.

So, I'm new to meditating... how do I do it?

It's easy. Clear your head of anything causing you stress and find a quiet place without distractions. Sit down, and get comfortable. Or, lie down. I'm also a fan of meditating while lying down (in addition to meditating during the day, I also meditate in bed when I wake up and when I fall asleep, but I digress).

Focus on your breathing. Inevitably, outside thoughts will distract you but just gently push those out of your mind. Try to avoid filling your mind with thoughts of, "Am I doing it right?" Simply relax and breathe and gently push away any thoughts that come to distract you.

If you're new to meditating, I would suggest you first try one of many widely available guided meditations. I have several that I use (some free, some purchased). Some good ones I like: Headspace, the Calm app, and anything by Deepak Chopra. My favorite Deepak Chopra meditation app is one he did with Oprah called "Desire & Destiny." It's a 21-day meditation series that you can rotate through again and again. It's outstanding and costs around $50.

I also use guided YouTube meditations. My favorite one on YouTube is called "*6 Phase Guided Mediation*" by Vishen Lakhiani. He gently guides you through a deep meditation focusing on love, kindness, gratitude, forgiveness, visualization and asking for divine guidance. Or, you can simply skip the guided mediations and choose to meditate alone, all by yourself.

When I first started meditating, I admit I wasn't great at it. One day I would have a great meditation experience and then other times I would be unable to clear my mind. I felt it was almost a waste of time. I couldn't stop thinking about something and focus on my breathing. Repeatedly, I would have to push the distracting thoughts away and re-center myself to the quiet. It was like musculature I had to flex and repeat over and over to make stronger. Today I can meditate for an hour or two at a time.

If you experience the same struggle, just keep at it until you get better and stronger at it. When you finally relax through meditation, it's worth it.

The results you will experience when you meditate include:

- You will learn to live more in the present moment.
- You will tap into your intuition.
- You will enjoy a mindset of positivity and gratitude.
- Your vibrational energy and frequency will increase.
- You will release low energies.
- You will experience alignment.

- You will have a peaceful Namaste outlook on life ("the light in me honors the light in you")
- We ground ourselves and align with a world that loves us.

If you've never experienced the benefits of meditation, trust me, give it a try. There is serious science supporting the benefits of meditating. I don't know even one person who has meditated regularly who has *not* noticed huge benefits. I know my life is more centered and I'm more aligned when I meditate. When I do it regularly, my life is in sync. When I don't, things don't go as well.

Meditation is also a great way to calm yourself when you have a stressful day and your mind is racing out of control. Five minutes of meditation can do wonders. It has taught me to see through the chaos of thought and fear so I can observe those emotions without getting involved. And better yet, when I began grounding myself for at least 5 minutes every day, I attracted people of a higher frequency with my new found Namaste attitude.

And you don't always have to be still when you're meditating. You don't even have to technically be meditating. You can have that silent connection while quietly doing the dishes at the kitchen sink, mowing the yard or ironing. One of my favorite things to do is muck horse stalls while centering myself and relaxing in the stillness and quiet.

There are other ways to experience mindfulness too: qigong yoga, tapping, energy work on your chakras, crystals, and through studying other spiritual paths such as *The Course in Miracles* and Taoism. Taoism is a Chinese philosophy that stresses the importance of humility and compassion and effortless action. The Tao de Ching stresses the following principles:

1. Simplicity.
2. Honesty.

3. Kindness.

4. Living a life of service.

5. Effortless action.

6. Living authentically.

7. Finding love in all things.

The world says I am what I have and what I have accomplished. The Tao says let go of everything. Less is more. Kindness and love is important. Simplicity is honored. And, gentleness is revered.

Here are some ways to bring Tao practices into your life, as another way to build a meditative practice through your day:

- Enjoy a relaxed cup of coffee or tea. Go to your favorite coffee shop and just sit and sip… don't check your phone or social media, leave your laptop at home, savor every moment, smell it, taste it.

- Consider ways you can live more minimally. We don't need more stuff; it doesn't bring lasting happiness.

- Slow down, don't rush. Take time to connect with someone.

Chapter 24
Step 7: Lean into the Discomfort – Feel It Through

Unfortunately, assholes bring a lot of negative energy into our lives. They enjoy instilling fear and insecurity and lots of other negative emotions when they are in their worst raging narcissist stage. We have to remind ourselves that we are beings of love, and not a part of negative energy and spirit of fear they bring. None of that comes from the universe. It all comes from your asshole. It's important to know how to respond and work to remain centered – admittedly it's hard to do if you're not ready for it. We'll fix that, sweet girl!

You'll be happy to know there is (what I call) a "magic threshold" to healing where you can conquer all that fear and negativity, and burn it up to the point it's released and gone. It requires facing the very uncomfortable.

It should first be pointed out that not all negative feelings are bad. They're a normal part of life and to be expected. They actually serve as guideposts in our life, letting us know when we're wobbling and out of alignment. These feelings alert us to make corrections and change our thinking. It's all part of discerning what your path is. They're guiding you. Lean into that!

Negative thoughts, however, become unhealthy when we hold on to them and they control us. When we find ourselves stuck ruminating on feelings of fear, confusion, insecurity, anger and sadness (the predominant "top 5" feelings we struggle with during and after narcissistic abuse) we're in trouble. That's when we know we have a problem and need to rid ourselves of all the negativity.

That's where the magic threshold comes in. And, I'll tell you exactly how to cross over that threshold. You just need to show up, and feel it all through… no matter how tough.

To rid yourselves of the negativity, you have to focus your attention on it fully and feel it. Let it burn up the old unwanted emotions… that is the threshold to healing! In detail, here's exactly how to do it (in this instance, let's consider the negative thought of fear):

1. Acknowledge it.

The first thing to do is acknowledge the fear. Yep, that awful thing happened, and yep, this other awful thing could happen to you, too. Acknowledge it. Embrace it. Don't deny the fear. Don't ignore it. Don't make it bigger than it is. Don't suppress it.

Be in a place of acceptance with it. I acknowledge it. I fear it, but I'm moving on. This is where I am now. But it's not where I have to stay.

2. Accept it.

Lean into it. Lean into the fear (or other negative feeling). Be in a place of surrender to its existence. It is what it is. Embrace that it's your reality. Let it settle in. You have no control over what has happened.

3. Feel it Through & Burn it up.

In the case of fear, feel the terror. Cry. Express indignation. Be angry. Livid. While in a safe place, express the feelings you have toward your asshole and flying monkeys. Share what you're feeling with trusted friends and family. Write in journal. These feelings need expression. Do it. You do not want to repress these feelings.

4. Release it… and determine what you want instead.

Release it! Turn it over to God (the universe). The next step is to determine "what do you want instead?"

Ask: *What do I want instead?*

Answer: *I want a life of no fear. I want someone who cherishes me and takes care of me and protects me. I want peace. I want real love. I want to be healthy, confident and free from worry for my safety and the safety of my children and family.*

Instead of focusing on the fear, focus on the opposite, i.e. focus on what you want in life. Remember, the law of attraction. What you focus on, expands and manifests.

Once we face our fears we take back our power to choose how we want to live our lives and when we do this, it changes our lives forever.

Worksheet #11

What are you ruminating about?

Imagine if you were focused instead only on mindfulness now!

Chapter 25
Step 8: Choose Your Drum Circle Carefully

"You are the average of the five people
you spend the most time with."
Jim Rohn

Jim Rohn was a genius business philosopher and motivational speaker who always spoke passionately about the importance of carefully choosing the people you surround yourself with. No truer words have ever been spoken than these above!

The people you spend the most time with, interact with, and do life with are the very people who influence you the most. They shape your habits, beliefs and how you live your life.

It's important to surround yourself with people who encourage and lift you up in healthy ways. Do you surround yourself with people who bring negativity into your life and discourage you (or worse yet, encourage you to live in an unhealthy manner)? Is there someone in your life who drains you emotionally with their pessimism and insists on hanging around? No one is entitled to take up room in your life. You decide who has access to you.

Take a time out now to examine who are the people and friends you spend the most time with. There are friends we *choose* to spend time with. There are coworkers and mentors we *must* associate with in our professional life. Do we have toxic family members who drain us with their negative and pessimistic outlook on life?

Now is the time to make changes to your circle of friends, your drum circle if you will, so they match up with your desire for a healthy and positive future moving forward. Be deliberate in choosing to spend more time with the people who encourage you in your plans to heal. Spend time with those people who help you gain strength and encourage you to be a better version of yourself and improve in areas where you want to improve. Say "no" to the people who encourage you to stay stuck in unhealthy patterns and say "yes" to those people who inspire you to reach for the stars.

And, it's not only the people around you that require a second look. The content and media that you choose to consume also has huge significance and impact in your life. Take a serious look at the books you're reading and the television shows you're watching. What type of content are you digesting? Is it encouraging to you? They say "Garbage in, garbage out." Is the content you're consuming inspiring, transformative, and motivating?

As part of creating the life you want to have, focus attention on learning and bettering yourself every day through the content you consume. Focus every day on personal growth including reading and writing. For me that meant doing a deep dive into reading books, listening to audio books and podcasts, watching YouTube videos, and talking with experts about self improvement and abuse recovery. Even today, when I'm at the gym, or taking my dog for a walk, when I'm working in the yard, when I'm cleaning, when I'm cooking and driving, I'm always listening to something that helps me learn.

Feed your mind and soul. Learn, learn, learn. Attend seminars, go to spiritual retreats, attend talks, read magazines. Or, maybe it's seeking out the knowledge, wisdom and experience of others who you trust. Having another perspective to learn from is invaluable. Feed your mind with all the things you're passionate about and that make you happy.

Make a habit every day to spend at least 30 minutes investing in yourself and feeding your mind something that will help you grow spiritually, physically, emotionally and mentally.

What are you passionate about?

What are your talents?

Do you have a dream of something you want to accomplish in your life?

What inspires you?

Who are the authors you love to read?

What do you wish you knew more about?

What do you feel led to listen to and learn more about?

Use the answers to these questions to direct you to areas and people to study. Indulge in those passions. I love audiobooks and consume and "read" books constantly. Maybe you prefer regular old-fashioned books? Choose whichever way you prefer to digest content, and go for it. I also prefer podcasts because I can listen when I'm busy about my day, and even when I'm sleeping (I know, crazy!). For the last three years, I have listened to favorite podcasts and audiobooks playing while I sleep and I wholeheartedly believe that those things have seeped into my subconscious because of that extra effort.

Here are the people I have spent the most time listening to and studying and whom have had the most influence on my healing in the past few years. **I promise you, you will be inspired if you** hear what they have to say. A lot of their material is free online (be sure to google them and visit their web sites), so you can learn more.

Brené Brown

I can't get enough of Brené Brown, can I just say that? She writes and speaks on topics of vulnerability, courage, authenticity, and shame - huge topics of interest and significance in my healing in the last couple of years. Every Ted talk I've watched of hers, every book of hers I've read, and every video I've seen her in have all resonated with me on so many levels. Quite simply, she's the cool-headed friend who makes the messy and complicated seem easy to navigate and she inspires me to live life fearlessly.

I loved hearing the story of her very first Ted talk (it's a must watch – find it by googling TEDxHouston "*The Power of Vulnerability*"). She gave that talk and then later worried aloud to a friend how embarrassed she was with her performance and how scared she was that her talk might possibly be uploaded online to where "up to 500 people" might see it - ha! The video WAS uploaded and it went viral. Today more than 32 million people have watched it.

Be sure to check out her Ted talks on YouTube (listed below), as well as her interviews with Oprah on YouTube (I love all of those – and you will, too!). And, connect with her on Twitter (@BreneBrown), Facebook and on her website (brenebrown.com). But by far, you will get the most from her books. I recommend starting with *Rising Strong.*

Brené's must-watch Ted talks:

TEDxHouston: The Power of Vulnerability

TED2012: Listening to Shame

My favorite Brené Brown books:

Braving the Wilderness: The Quest for True Belonging and the Courage to Stand Alone

Rising Strong: How the Ability to Reset Transforms the Way We Live, Love, Parent, and Lead

Daring Greatly: How the Courage to Be Vulnerable Transforms the Way We Live, Love, Parent, and Lead

The Gifts of Imperfection: Let Go of Who You Think You're Supposed to Be and Embrace Who You Are

My favorite Brené Brown quotes:

> "The middle is messy, but it's also where the magic happens."
>
> Brené Brown

> "Vulnerability is about showing up and being seen. It's tough to do that when we're terrified about what people might see or think."
>
> *Brené Brown*

Tony Robbins:

You surely have been living under a rock or have zero interest in self-improvement if you've never heard of Tony Robbins. He's the best... really fantastic if you're looking to work on yourself. I can't tell you how many hours I have spent mowing and exercising, driving, cooking, cleaning and more while listening to his audio CDs. A few years ago I spent an insane amount of money buying as many of his self-improvement audio courses that I could, and I have since devoured them again and again. They are *that* good. He simply has the best advice and outlook on making changes in your life.

He's an author, entrepreneur, and life coach who is known for his self-help books and seminars. I understand something like 50 million people have benefited from his teachings. I consider him to *the* rock-star top-dog motivational speaker of all (although he shuns that label of "motivational speaker"). As I mentioned before, I had the honor of working with him and interviewing him a few years ago. I never took him up on his invitation to attend one of his seminars… dumb move on my part, not finding the time to do that! I will never forget what I learned from him though during that interview... amazing man!

What you need to know about Tony is he's a "Why" guy. WHY do you do what you do? WHY do you do what you DON'T want to do? WHY does your partner do what he/she does? He takes a serious deep dive into human decision-making and how we can make changes to better our lives through changing our actions. It might sound a little woo-woo at a high level to some, but his programs and teaching materials are fantastic. I most recently did Tony's 10-day audio course called "*Creating Lasting Change*." I've gone through it twice and highly recommend it.

Also, at the printing of this, Tony has a TV documentary out called "*I Am Not Your Guru - Tony Robbins*." That will give you a flavor of what he offers. Also, there are tons of (free) Tony Robbins videos on YouTube. There are hours and hours of videos to watch. Again, sleep to his materials and you'll be digesting great positive content as your subconscious mind takes it in.

Cliff Ravenscraft:

If you haven't heard of Cliff Ravenscraft yet and you're into self-improvement, trust me you will be hearing a lot more about this man. He's quickly becoming the most sought-after personal improvement coach out there who specializes in resetting your mindset (… *hello, you're speaking my language!)*. He has done more to inspire me to make positive changes in my life in recent years than probably all the influencers listed here combined... in areas of health & wellness, business development, personal growth, all of it.

What I love about Cliff is he is real and authentic and while he is all about results and making hard progress and making decisive changes, he is completely relatable. He offers practical advice on "doing life" and growing and improving, but he doesn't do it in a Tony Robbins Mach-3 level "attack at 5000-RPM" kind of approach. Some days I don't want to examine the reasons WHY people do what they do, or how my life conditions don't match my blueprint, or what new "empowering alternatives" or action items I can create for myself. Some days I'm just trying to make it through the day, one baby step at a time. Sometimes I just want a bag of Pepperidge Farm Double Milanos, a soft blanket and my pillow. I want balance. Something tells me if I told Cliff I was having that kind of day, he wouldn't crucify me. He feels infinitely more relatable than Tony Robbins on those days (*sorry, Tony*). Quite simply, Cliff inspires me to be a better person, mom, friend, and business owner and to enjoy the journey along the way (*sigh*).

To get a taste of what he's all about, check out Cliff Ravenscraft's YouTube channel. You will hear his take on how to deal with self-doubt, kick-starting your mindset, staying focused, saying "no" and lots of other topics. He used to focus on helping people launch their own podcasts (hence his nickname, the "Podcast Answer Man"), but has since made the decided shift to helping people take their lives and businesses to the next level.

My favorite Cliff Ravenscraft quote:

> "I don't need easy. I just need worth it."
>
> *Cliff Ravenscraft*

Hal Elrod:

You already know I'm a huge fan of Hal's **book,** *The Miracle Morning: The Not-So-Obvious Secret Guaranteed to Transform Your Life Before 8AM.* It will kick-start your life. Get it, read it, establish a new morning routine and get on with your life. But his podcast is also a must-listen-to. It's called Hal Elrod's *Achieve Your Goals Podcast.*

My favorite Hal Elrod quote:

> "Remember, the moment you accept total responsibility for everything in your life is the moment you claim the power to change anything in your life."
>
> *Hal Elrod*

Wayne Dyer (1940-2015)

Wayne Dyer has taught me almost everything I know about how our thoughts control our lives and manifest what we want (and don't want) in our lives. If I were you, I would subscribe today to his podcast and start listening. And, listen to anything you can find on YouTube of him speaking. Or watch his PBS specials. He's wonderful, and although he passed years ago I'm grateful we still have his talks to listen to.

My favorite Wayne Dyer books:

Change Your Thoughts - Change Your Life: Living the Wisdom of the Tao

The Power of Intention

My favorite Wayne Dyer quotes:

> "If you change the way you look at things, the things you look at change."
>
> *Wayne Dyer*

> "Abundance is not something we acquire. It is something we tune into."
>
> *Wayne Dyer*

Anita Moorjani:

My favorite Ted talk of all time is hands-down Anita Moorjani's talk at

TEDxBayArea "*Dying to Be Me.*" After I watched this Ted talk, I started following Anita on Facebook and elsewhere and read her book by the same name, *Dying to Be Me.* I love the lessons she teaches: we are all connected to one another, we are all love, our internal life & dialogue are the keys to happiness, the outer world is distracting and not something we should react to, and if we are at peace, then the world will reflect that back to us.

Be sure to watch the Ted talk and hear her story of almost dying, seeing the "other side" and coming back to share what she learned. Everyone I have shared the link with has loved it.

My favorite Anita Moorjani quotes:

> "Transform your world by transforming your internal state. Start by learning to let go of negative self-judgment, and replace it with positive and loving thoughts about yourself. Be kind to yourself, and watch your external world change."
>
> *Anita Moorjani*

> "Your only purpose is to be yourself, otherwise you deprive the universe of who you came here to be."
>
> *Anita Moorjani*

Billy Graham:

Honestly, Billy Graham perhaps should rank #1 at the top of this list of influencers, now that I think about it. :-)

You know when you're hurting and sick and need nourishing comfort food, rest and an assurance that you can find the right path forward that your intuition confirms is the right way? That's what Billy Graham has provided for me in my healing. He's one of the great spiritual teachers in my life. When I need healing, am at loss as to what to do, or am feeling hopeless, he has been my go-to source for trustworthy, wholesome, nourishing sustenance. Even as a parent, I remember one occasion with my son (when he was probably about 10 years old) sitting him down in front of my laptop and playing a Billy Graham sermon for him after he misbehaved. Billy Graham was my last resort that day - ha!

As we all know, Billy Graham has preached the message of Christ's forgiveness and redemption for years and he's known for being a kind and non-judgmental man. We need more men like that. My best advice for getting some BG wisdom quickly is to simply go to YouTube and search "Billy Graham sermons"... hours of good stuff!

Chapter 26
Step 9: Don't Tap the Brakes – Be Authentically You

So, yeah, if your journey has been anything like mine, you've dealt with lots of fear in your life. And, I've learned one thing through my journey: the antidote to fear is to do something. Do something that challenges you. They say a comfort zone is a beautiful place to be, but nothing ever grows there. Most people avoid discomfort at any cost. But you can't grow if you don't challenge yourself. If you're unhappy in an area of your life, if you want a different life, you're going to have to do something that challenges you and usually that means facing one of your fears.

I believe one of our greatest fears – having come from a place where we have completely hidden and lost ourselves appeasing and pleasing our assholes – is using our voice and expressing ourselves. One of the things that scares us most is getting comfortable again, revealing who we really are… Our story. Our shame. The real you. What you like. What you find beautiful. What you fear. What you struggle with. The ugly, the beautiful. The simple, the complex. The funny, the sad. All of it.

Your purpose in life is to simply be you… fully and authentically you!

And, the easiest way to get back to you is to express yourself creatively every day. No longer being silent. No longer ashamed. No longer being afraid of what other people think. Every day fearlessly embracing the experience and never tapping the brakes. Go all-in expressing yourself for the purpose of getting back in touch with you.

And, you don't have to be "a creative" to do this. Maybe for you this means journaling every day. I recently found a journal that I started a few years ago when I was traveling and I was writing in it every day. It's a treasure to read through it now. If journaling isn't for you, consider painting or doodling every day or start a blog or a 365 project. Create music, write song lyrics, paint, write poetry. Or, simply find something beautiful every day and take a picture of it with your phone's camera. You will find being creative and expressing yourself increases your sense of well-being.

You don't even have to share your creations with anyone or make your work public. But every day, just find something creative to compose. Maybe it's a photo or a note to somebody or something amazing you cook. Just create something and in some way, express yourself. In doing so, you will be exercising freedom and being authentic and will be in a good mood because it's fun. Sadly, most people play it safe and small, and tell themselves they can't express themselves creatively. They worry and have no faith, only fear… no love.

Happiness comes from embracing you, and the "now." Happiness is in not letting moments pass you by. It's about the power of now and finding joy in the journey, because there really is no destination. The journey is everything. And expressing the real you to the world along the journey is everything.

Even if you feel nervous about expressing yourself, the "risk" you perceive it to be will make you feel more alive and will put you in a state of flow where you feel amazing. You will experience what it feels like to be in the moment, completely absorbed in what you're expressing. Have you ever done something that left you feeling more alive than ever before? High in flow, trusting in the universe, expressing our true selves, that's when we're in alignment and at our best! If you want security, go to prison. If you want freedom and a new-found peace, express yourself creatively every day.

Writing this book was one of the riskiest, scariest things I've done in my life. But I have never felt more alive and more in alignment spiritually, emotionally, mentally and physically. I know not every moment will I feel in alignment, but I'm growing… and continuing to grow. I'm no longer hiding and afraid. I'm following my own path, and am a stronger version of myself. I'm being who I authentically am meant to be. And, you can be a stronger version of yourself simply by following your own unique path. Choose to fearlessly be YOU moving forward, with no looking back.

Chapter 27
Step 10: Radically Ridiculously Forgive

Before you get a bee in your bonnet and go crazy on me over the thought of discussing forgiveness toward your asshole, let me first say a few things…

First, I get it. I've been there. I've seen people in my life do things that I personally would never do. It's beyond anyone's imagination how they could do what they did. And, I'm sure you're the same. You can't believe how horrible your person has been. Raised as you were, with standards of right and wrong and your value system, you would NEVER do what they chose to do, ever. Flat out, it's wrong!

And while I get that, I need to share with you a way I learned of dealing with those people where I walked away feeling nothing but love for them and no longer allowed them to affect me or cover me with their negative energy. I admit I have no control over whether they regret what they did or if they would still do the same thing again, but I do have control over how I deal with it.

So, listen, I'll make this short and sweet because this is a rather simple concept to convey and explain. And, I know you're not going to like what I'm about to say, but you've got to hear it:

It's only through forgiveness that we find peace. There's no other way.

In order to fully heal you're going to have to buck it up and learn about this thing called "radical ridiculous forgiveness."

This is no wimsy-wamsy half-hearted tongue-in-cheek forgiveness. This is a "meat and potatoes" powerful life-changing forgiveness that will be foundational to your healing.

And, by the way, this is something you work on *during* your healing, not after. Lots of people think forgiveness is an act and feeling that comes only *after* you work through healing from trauma. Some say it's not even possible to forgive when you're still angry and upset and feelings are still raw. Nope.

Hanging on to anger and resentment has a devastating negative impact upon your spiritual and emotional life. It's only through forgiveness that we can be truly in alignment with God and the universe and heal. When we choose to forgive others for their transgressions, that's adhering to love and is evidence that our heart is pure and spiritually mature.

It doesn't mean he didn't do what he did. It doesn't mean that he didn't harm us. It doesn't mean our flying monkeys didn't do what they did. Forgiveness is *not* about pretending all the bad stuff never happened. It doesn't mean all those things are okay and not-a-big deal. And, you don't need to "forgive & forget" (nor should you).

The goal here is letting go and getting right with the universe. It's about releasing all negative emotions toward your asshole and flying monkeys and no longer letting them have a hold on you. When you boil it down, it's about exercising mercy.

Forgiveness doesn't deny or lessen the gravity of what happened. Forgiveness is granting to your asshole and flying monkeys something they don't deserve. It's about letting go of the need to punish them yourself. It's about choosing love (and mercy) over justice. And, that pleases the universe. That, pleases God.

Try as you might, you cannot forget what happened. That's hard to do. But, here's how to profoundly and deeply forgive your asshole and flying monkeys. Stop yourself the next time you hear yourself ruminating on their wrong-doing and saying/feeling the following sentiments:

"That person shouldn't have done that."

"That was wrong."

"That person is bad."

"That's one evil person right there."

Stop for a minute and be real.

You weren't raised like them. Your own experiences brought you to where you are today, and your experiences are different from theirs. The truth is, IF you have been raised like them, had every one of their experiences that brought them to where they are today, it's possible to imagine that you, too, may have actually made the very same poor decision they made.

That could have been you right there having done the same thing(s). It's not even just possible, it might even be likely that you would have made the *exact same* decision they made. It's really that simple. You may have done the same thing.

By changing my perspective of how I looked at them and what they did and why they did it and having empathy that I could have been them, all the negative feelings disappeared. Poof. I felt instantly free. There was nothing to have angst about. All the condemnation and resentment and animosity just disappeared. The negative energy turned into a loving energy and that resounded within my soul.

Inevitably, when dealing with an asshole, you will see some unbelievable ugliness (aggression, anger, selfishness, lying) and it really hurts. When I was going through my "stuff," one of my flying monkeys fabricated a story, accusing me and my son of stalking her. It was not true, and after thousands of dollars spent having to fight off the accusations in court, a judge dismissed the accusations adding, "no credible evidence was presented." The entire episode was traumatizing for me and my son.

It took me a long time to get past the anger and indignation of what happened. But, I finally learned how to look upon her with love, instead of anger through exercising radical ridiculous forgiveness.

I had to admit to myself, IF I had been raised as she was, and had the same experiences that she had, it's possible that I, too, could have felt pressured to make the same wrong decisions that she made.

I was able to walk away feeling love for her. I was able to forgive her without prejudice and without receiving an apology. I chose love. I chose forgiveness in spite of what she did. I chose empathy and kindness. My light shines brighter for it. I love harder today because of having gone through that experience. Her darkness can't hurt me anymore. I choose to not hold her behavior against her anymore. Showing mercy and love is a wonderful thing. And further, the forgiveness allowed me to refuse to ruminate on it any longer.

I chose to focus those ruminating thoughts on positivity instead. And when I'm ever tempted to ruminate on what happened, I deliberately choose to refocus on something else. I release the negative thoughts and negative energy.

It's important to forgive independently of whether or not our asshole (or flying monkeys) apologize for their actions. It's also good to forgive independently of whether or not we believe they are sincere when we do receive an apology. We agree to love them fully regardless.

Chapter 28
Step 11: Don't React, Choose Love

This is the one final step that will, by far, have the most impact in changing your life.

The next time your asshole or flying monkey (or anyone in your life, for that matter) does something upsetting and you're ready to fly in to action and respond with a dish of exactly what they deserve, I need you to pause.

Yes, I know you want to text him right now. You want to pick up the phone and give that person a piece of your mind. I know you want to tell everyone about the absurdity and depravity of what they did. You want to vent. You're extremely upset, I can see that. But spewing out our feelings causes us to do things we later regret. And the biggest thing we will regret as we fly off the track of alignment is that we immediately deflect all miracles coming our way.

You need to reject the urge to react. Don't act. Stop. Take your hands off the wheel, in other words.

Remain still. The Bible says, "Be still" (Psalm 46:10). Stop. Release it. Submit yourself. Doing nothing is where the miracles happen. When you step back and let the universe handle it, that's when the good things come.

Don't write that email. Don't text him. Don't let your pissed off heart pick up the phone to call him. You're in charge here. And, by the way, be careful of friends around you who tell you to "do it, do it, do it!" It's far better to do nothing. Trust the universe and it will guide you to what you want.

Don't deflect the miracles coming your way. God is our refuge and our strength. Trust that.

Instead, always respond in love. Always choose love. When you choose love, you choose not to deflect the miracles. Every time you don't react in fear and anger and instead choose to respond in love, you diffuse the hate. The more love you give, the more you have in your life.

Conclusion

In the end, it's a process. The healing will continue. We can't change what happened in the past. We can only remove ourselves from the reach of people who don't value our heart.

I am still healing and still have a way to go, but I am a long way from where I was. Going through all I did, I learned so much about myself and have become a woman I'm proud to be. I have found wonderful, powerful new friendships with others who have traveled (and are traveling now) on the same journey. I have become spiritually grounded and focused intently on what's important in life. I have peace in my life. I've gained confidence – more so than I ever had before. I love myself and all others more than I ever have before. While I can never undo what happened to me, or eradicate the bad memories, I feel proud to have taken control of my life and be moving forward in a direction that is guided by inspiration and passion. Above all, I am relieved to be free.

Today, I simply want to be happy and live in the present. From now on, I will be grateful for all I have. I will make choices carefully. Yes, I still get upset at times, as we all do, but I never stay there.

No more settling for a relationship where I receive more confusion and hurt than love. No more settling for a relationship that depletes my spirit more than it empowers me. I have strong boundaries now. I won't do anything I know isn't in alignment. I won't *be* with anyone who isn't in alignment, either.

The truth is, today I feel sorry for my asshole, because he had everything and let it all slip through his fingers. We had a shot at a healthy relationship, and he blew it. I overlooked his flaws and his temper and still chose him. I invested everything in him. He was never satisfied, even with my beating heart in the very palm of his hand. Now, all he is to me is a source of profound sadness. He's not the strong man I once believed him to be. But, I forgive him. And, I'm proud of myself for being strong enough to survive what was I was dealt. What I feel for him is not anger, not bitterness, just sadness. And love. I will always love him and hold out hope that he finds himself. Not for me, but for him. I have moved on. I hope, with all my heart, he and his flying monkeys do the same.

It's funny how life sorts out in the end for the greater good. There really is a thing called karma, I've learned. Today, my son is happy and safe and doing well. He's attending his first year of college on a full ride scholarship due to his efforts speaking out against domestic violence and the nightmare we lived through. Also, my trusted attorney who was by my side every step of the awful way through my ordeal, was recently appointed by our state's Governor to be a judge. He now oversees other cases of domestic abuse and women seeking protection. I can't think of a more honorable, worthy and just man to sit on the bench and protect the interests of victims.

And, I have a greater purpose now. My goal now is to help women victimized by all forms of abuse (financial, emotional, physical and more). I want to help those who have lost themselves in a toxic relationship and feel wounded to the point they believe they have no voice and no power to overcome their situation. I want them to take the same journey I took and grow stronger through the ordeal. Not weaker. Today I see myself as the strong and beautiful woman I am. I'm victorious.

Have you ever seen someone with a semi colon tattoo? I didn't know until very recently what a semicolon symbolized. Come to find out, its universal meaning is quite lovely.

Project Semicolon is an organization that was founded to "Present hope and love to those struggling with depression, suicide, addiction, and self-injury." *Project Semicolon* invites people to wear a semicolon tattoo to show they are committed to moving forward despite troubles. The semicolon represents a movement to bring people together, to empower each other and prove that we can all overcome obstacles we face. It represents we can all rewrite the ending to our story and reset our lives no matter how desperate and hopeless we feel. We can all start over. We have the strength to keep fighting even during the bleakest moments. We have the power to heal. Love and goodness will be victorious in the end.

I know I deserve to be with someone whose heart is led to protect me and do whatever it takes to be a true partner with me. I now know that I deserve to be with someone who is always going to prioritize my well-being; someone who doesn't take advantage, someone who doesn't feed into my insecurities or fear, someone deserving of my loyalty and devotion. I know I am deserving of someone who will never capitalize on my weaknesses. I know I deserve someone who is going to bring out the best in both of us, someone who makes our relationship stronger.

I simply want to be happy and I look at where I am today, and I am.

Years ago I wrote a lifestyle feature article for Scripps Howard News Service that was distributed to hundreds of newspapers across the country. It was about "happiness" and specifically asked and answered the question, "What makes us all happy?"

I interviewed experts and authors and mental health professionals and the findings were this: spiritual faith, community, having goals, enjoying good health, and financial stability are all important areas of well-being leading to a happy life.

Advice offered in the article as to "how to get happy," was as follows:

Stop complaining. Venting and whining often has the opposite effect. Research shows that rumination increases sadness and decreases motivation. Resist the urge to vent and challenge yourself to not complain.

Focus on the positive & let it go. Persistent negative thoughts can contribute to depression. For every negative situation, look for a positive. If there is no silver lining in a circumstance, let it go. Realize you cannot control everything.

Give. Give of time and money. It's not so much the amount of money or complexity of the act. It's the act itself of giving to another person. This strengthens social connections and builds a bond with the person to whom you are giving. Simple acts of kindness — preparing a meal for someone, lending an ear to a friend in crisis, writing a letter, all return huge dividends to the person giving.

Buy "experiences." A short-term boost can be had from buying "things," but you get a longer term boost from buying "experiences." One reason for that, is we re-live those experiences, and forge stronger social connections through experiences with other people. Taking a vacation, having a cup of coffee with a friend, attending a musical performance with a loved one, are all ways to create memories.

Get moving. Exercise doesn't have to mean pushing yourself to extremes in the gym. Do something that increases your heart rate and sounds fun to you: walking your dog, gardening, tennis, sex – all of these things release endorphins and make us feel good.

Savor the simple things in life. It's said the best things in life are free. Take notice and embrace those every day simple pleasures in life: the sounds of chirping birds, fresh air, beautiful sunsets.

Stop procrastinating. Spend time every day tackling a project or task you've been putting off. Feelings of accomplishment will encourage you to complete other projects lurking on your to-do list.

Surround yourself with happy people. Have you noticed happy people seem to make those around them happy? Indeed, happiness begets happiness. And if you're not feeling happy, act happy. Put a smile on your face. The feelings will follow.

Start a gratitude journal. Count your blessings and write about them. Studies show people who focus on what they are thankful for are far happier than those who don't.

Don't expect to be happy at all times. It's normal to experience the natural ebb and flow of feelings of happiness. It's okay to feel sad or overwhelmed. Those feelings are part of life.

Set goals. In all important areas of your life (physical, financial, professional, home, relationships, and fun), set goals and develop plans for reaching those goals. Seek advice from trusted friends and mentors for guidance, and then get started!

Pamper yourself. Carve out time to relax and unwind. Take a bubble bath. Recline in a hammock and read a book. Buy yourself flowers. You deserve it!

Most importantly, according to the experts I interviewed in that article, our happiness is under our control! Science shows *we* have the power to affect positive change in our lives and create happiness.

I will always remain focused on my healing and continuing to get stronger. I have compassion for those people who have caused me harm and I thank them for being the source of my greatest spiritual awakening. I really do thank them. I'm free today.

I'm free from being intimidated by any posse of flying monkeys.

I'm free from being hopelessly in love with someone incapable of having a healthy relationship.

I'm free from having to remind myself I'm worth something and that my happiness counts too.

I'm free from panic attacks.

I'm free from gas-lighting.

I'm free from reading and googling behavior that I see and don't understand.

I'm free from ruminating, reliving and rehashing ugliness.

I'm free from being made to financially struggle.

I'm free from walking on eggshells.

I'm free from feeling like I've done something wrong.

I'm free from the horror of having my heart broken when it was supposed to have been 100% safe in the hands of someone I loved.

I'm free from betrayal.

I'm free from waiting for an apology I will never receive.

I'm free to live my life without fear.

I'm free to live in peace.

I'm free to live with joy and happiness.

I'm free to follow my heart.

I'm free to fulfill my purpose in this world.

I'm free to be who God made me to be.

I'm free in knowing I am beautiful and spirit-filled.

I'm free to trust my intuition.

I'm free to hopefully inspire others to be free.

And, I'm free to know I deserve so much better.

I'm truly free. I've never felt more free than I do today.

Now, it's your turn, sweet girl! Free yourself!

You can do it. I love you and believe in you.

10 Commandments for Surviving an Asshole

(set of principles to help you survive and heal from this toxic relationship)

1. Trust your intuition.
2. Don't ignore red flags.
3. Set boundaries and stick to them.
4. Don't succumb to fear.
5. Continually purify your mind and body and meditate daily.
6. Thought by thought choose alignment.
7. Ignore the flying monkeys.
8. Stay connected to source, God, the universe, the divine, whatever you choose to call it.
9. Lean into the discomfort and feel it through, no matter how tough.
10. Fully accept this struggle and pain as the source of your greatest spiritual awakening.

Okay, 10 More Commandments

1. Always be authentically you.
2. Don't judge yourself by what your asshole did to you.
3. Feel the feelings of having what you desire.
4. Choose to live at a higher frequency. *Don't take on another person's lower vibrational energy and then blame them for your lack of peace.*
5. You're not lost. Your authentic self is simply buried. Uncover it and love it.
6. Never give up.
7. Don't force anything.
8. Pay attention to messages from the universe.
9. Stay grounded in love, i.e. have a Namaste outlook on life ("… the light in me honors the light in you…").
10. Radically ridiculously forgive.

My Biggest Lessons Learned

Needless to say, I've learned so many lessons through my healing. Here are the 23 biggest lessons I've learned along the way:

- Some people who you thought were dear friends will reveal themselves to be flying monkeys and will do horrific things to hurt you. Other casual friends will hurt you by being politically correct and not wanting to take sides, giving your abuser a pass. They don't understand the harm they are doing and that by not standing up against abuse, they are emboldening abusers.
- How others treat you is their path. How you choose to respond is yours.
- People will do to you what you allow them to do to you. Never allow anyone to mistreat you. Don't tolerate disrespect.
- Friends and family will not understand what you've been through. They will tell you to "just get over it" or "it couldn't have been that bad if you stayed as long as you did." Other people will accuse you of lying and will ridicule you. You will be re-traumatized all over again when this happens. During a time when you most need support, some people are ignorant to narcissistic abuse. Their poor choices and ignorance are not a reflection on you. And it really doesn't matter anyway. Focus on you

and your healing.

- Narcissistic and domestic abuse is happening all around you every day. People you are close to are hiding abuse and sadness. Be sensitive to the plight of these people. They may be barely hanging on.
- A counselor or therapist trained in trauma and PTSD is of huge help in healing from an abusive experience.
- Your instinct is accurate – always listen to it. That's the universe talking to you.
- Facebook memories suck sometimes.
- When I meditate daily, life is better. When I don't meditate daily, not so much.
- Fear and shame can be crushing and debilitating. Shame makes us stay quiet, afraid to let even our closest friends know the truth due to fear of embarrassment, fear of ridicule, fear of losing our relationship, fear of retaliation from our asshole. Never allow fear to cripple you from moving forward.
- Never be bullied into silence. If someone tries to silence you, speak up louder. Seek the help you need to be free from abuse.
- There is never anything to worry about. Either we have control over a situation or we don't. If we do, then take control and change the situation. If we don't, then we need to forget about it. Worrying won't help anything. There is therefore nothing to worry about, ever. Fretting over things we can't control is a complete waste of time.
- When I stay emotionally centered in peace and aligned and choose love instead of fear and negativity, miracles happen in my life and everything works out for my greatest good.

- Sharing and talking about your story helps you heal.
- Never ignore red flags.
- Changing who you are at your core in order to please someone you love is not love. Never change who you are. The person who truly loves you will want you to be your authentic self. Be yourself and don't change. Be strong and calm, and hold your ground.
- You have no control of an asshole's actions (their anger, their decisions, etc.).
- Don't ever define yourself by what others do to you. Their actions and their opinions are theirs, and not for you to take any ownership in. I am beautiful and strong and bigger and bolder than the hurt inflicted on me.
- Flying monkeys are the most horrifying aspect to leaving a narcissist.
- Healing takes time. Be patient.
- After leaving the relationship you will have no desire to date. Victims never do. You will be slow to trust again. Your abuser on the other hand will quickly replace you. He needs supply and he will get it where he can. This is textbook narcissist behavior.
- The abuse never ends when the relationship ends.
- I am stronger than I ever realized.

Recommended books to read:

- *Boundaries: When to Say Yes, How to Say No to Take Control of Your Life* by Dr. Henry Cloud and Dr. John Townsend
- *Daring Greatly: How the Courage to Be Vulnerable Transforms the Way We Live, Love, Parent and Lead* by Brené Brown
- *Divorcing a Narcissist: Advice from the Battlefield* by Tina Swithin
- *Dying to be Me: My Journey from Cancer, to Near Death, to True Healing*, Anita Moorjani
- *The Gifts of Imperfection: Let Go of Who You Think You're Supposed to Be and Embrace Who You Are by* Brené Brown
- *Girl, Wash Your Face: Stop Believing the Lies About Who You Are So You Can Become Who You Were Meant to Be* by Rachel Hollis
- *God is Able* by Priscilla Shirer
- *Happy You, Happy Body: 6 Easy Steps to Creating Your Happy Body* by Karen Jones
- *Love Hurts: Buddhist Advice for the Heartbroken* by Lodro Rinzler
- *The Miracle Morning: The 6 Habits That Will Transform Your Life Before 8AM* by Hal Elrod

- *Modern Man in Search of a Soul* by Carl Jung
- *The Power of Your Subconscious Mind* by Joseph Murphy
- *Rising Strong: How the Ability to Reset Transforms the Way We Live, Love, Parent and Lead* by Brené Brown
- *Strengths Finder 2.0* by Tom Rath
- *The Subtle Art of Not Giving a F*ck* by Mark Manson
- *The Universe Has Your Back: Transform Fear to Faith* by Gabrielle Bernstein
- *The Untethered Soul: The Journey Beyond Yourself* by Michael Singer
- *The War of Art: Breakthorugh the Blocks and Win Your Inner Creative Battles* by Steven Pressfield
- *Well Being: The Five Essential Elements* by Tom Rath & Jim Harter
- *What You Want Wants You* by Thomas Bahler
- *Why Does He Do That?* by Lundy Bancroft
- *Year of Yes* by Shonda Rhimes
- *You Are a Badass* by Jen Sincero

ACKNOWLEDGMENTS

Thank you to those who have helped me the most in my healing: Matt Sharpsteen, Duke & Ann Woodhull (Mom & Dad), Mack McKeller, Marlaine Belanger, Cliff Ravenscraft, Jodi Miller, Anne Meijers, Tandy Cannon, and Sunshine – my sweet friend and business partner (let's go do this!).

Gratitude to our amazing team for helping to get this book and message to the finish line: Sharon McTurk (you are such a blessing!), KG, Brother Bear, Brown Cow, Big Scallop, Susannah Furr, Kaine Mccalister, Susan S. Dickman, John R Buric at JAMES, McELROY & DIEHL P.A., C. Christopher Clark, Esq., and Debra L Feit.

Thank you to the men in my life who prove there are good and true men in the world: Ben Sharpsteen, Jim McCammon, Ed Coye, Tommy Bahler and Spero Theros.

Thank you to those who helped me during difficult times: Sheriff David Mahoney, Bennett Greenberg, David Joyce, Helene & Marvin Gralnick, Eva Smith, Bob & Bev Jason, Phillip Jarret, Tony Austin, Nola-Ann Ven Hearden & Andrew, Patty Fisk, Patti Butler, Isabelle von Losch, Jim & Cindy Saba and Royle & Judith Duff.

My loving circle of friends: Andrew Hamilton, Makemie Scoville, Joyce Douglas, Patty Merrell, Christy Davis, Nancy & Chip Scardo, Steve & Anne Kendrick, Ty & Kady Hendrix, Jimmy Harris, Elayne Sheridan &

Dennis DeVore, Mark Weinstein & Susan Marsee, Dema Barishnikov, Billy Smith, Paul & Ann Buchman, Johannes & Liz Klapdohr, Patti Beggs, Gina Sanders, Ed & Marie Mettler, Al & Carol Horrigan, Beth McTeer, Debra Persinger, Jeanette Lee, Maureen Murphy, Teri Olsen, Molly Tartt, Dian Brewton, Vickie Carpenter, Sharon Jenkins, Debbie West, Portia Odell, Brenda Monk, Sandy Briggs, Kathy Haehnel, Eve Gregg, Lawson Turner & Lauren Stallings, Ed Belanger, Derek Belanger, Morgan Beck, Joanne Krause, Duke & Lisa Parrish, Gus Napier, Jennifer Burgin, Keturah Algood & Carolyn Bane, Bonnie Palmer, Corrine ("Charvi") Hadley, Lisa Patty Abbey, Don Debiase, Faith Malloy, Stan Moress, Ravi Pendse, Al & Sally Buch, Nola Jackson, Horst Stahl & Gabriele Jung, Kevin Bidwell, Marcy Thompson, "Niki" Anne-Monique Ransdel and Sonia Araripe & the rest of my Brazilian family.

Thank you to the following amazing women who inspire me: Karen Jones, Sophia Cooke, Stephanie Ravenscraft

How to Reach Ann

Web site: annsharpsteen.com

Twitter: @annsharpsteen

Facebook: Ann Sharpsteen

Instagram: @annsharpsteen

For speaking engagements, please email booking@annsharpsteen.com

Sending love to all of you.

Matt & Ann

Made in the USA
Coppell, TX
03 August 2023

19930156R00121